925 msc ✓

66 [struck through]

910·4

AUTHOR MARRINER, J

TITLE MARINER IN THE MEDITERRANEAN

D0119754

101 134 214 10

MARINER IN THE MEDITERRANEAN

by the same author
Afloat in Europe

Mariner
IN THE
Mediterranean

BY JOHN MARRINER

ADLARD COLES LIMITED

WANDSWORTH PUBLIC LIBRARIES

First published in book form in 1967 by
Adlard Coles Ltd, 1–3 Upper James
Street, London W1, and printed in Great
Britain by W. & J. Mackay & Co Ltd,
Chatham, Kent © John Marriner 1967.

D027342

910.4.MAR

for

Argo, Barracuda, Carrina, Cherryl II, Chinta, Clonsilla, Diana Loraine, Escaper, Explorer, Fantasia, Herald, Jason, Mawingo, Odyssey, Selemat, Selene, Voyageur

and all the other small boats whose friendship has helped me understand our comrade the sea

Acknowledgements

I would like to acknowledge the kindness of the Editors of *The Yachting World*, *Yachting Monthly*, and *The Yachtsman* for allowing me to make use of material that has already appeared in their magazines.

But quite especially I offer my grateful thanks to Frank Snoxell, at that time in the editorial chair of *The Motor Boat and Yachting*, and who first had the courage to put my yachting tales into print, and to Erroll Bruce, his successor in that chair, for his help and encouragement to go ahead with this book.

Contents

List of Illustrations

List of Maps

Foreword

To start with . . .

I ought to explain that, having done most of continental Europe in my boat and really got rather bored with the so-called 'yachting' that goes on along the South Coast of France and those parts, I decided to get right away from it all. At least, at that time, you could have called it that. Since then, of course, the Aegean, Adriatic and those parts are like Piccadilly Circus. Still, this book may help those who, like me, want to get further away from it all.

1
Getting away from it all

'September Tide' moves off, via Italy and Yugoslavia,
to a new base in Greece

By the end of the 1960 season I was once more in that congested area known as the French Riviera. For years I had found myself cruising in the classic waters of the Barcelona–Naples range, including Corsica, the Balearics and the northern tip of Sardinia. Everyone should see these places from a yacht at least once, but one can also have too much of them. The local yachting base—which I suppose one must concede to be either Cannes or Monaco—has, furthermore, become so difficult to enjoy, due principally to the gross overcrowding which the authorities seem to do nothing to alleviate (not to mention the obvious abuses which accompany such things) that a serious cruising yacht must find little to attract her to these shores.

Whither then? To return to the charms of the Baltic—even if one did not already know them—might seem too far. The obvious solution was to go south and get away from it all by wintering either in Malta or Piraeus, the two newest places in the yachtsman's calendar.

It was already September. The prophets were saying, 'Take care.' One often heard, 'The equinoctial gales are near.' There was no lack of Cassandras to warn of the perils of the Adriatic and Aegean late in the season. But *September Tide* had already taken it green many times that season in the Gulf of Lions and off Toulon. So we faced the future calmly.

Our first leg was a long one—from Villefranche, which we left one lunch-time, to Porto Ferraio, in the island of Elba—a distance of exactly 100 sea-miles. This is an easy passage navigationally, especially at night, since one can pick up the big light on Giraglia Island, at the northern tip

of Corsica, some 20 miles off in clear weather, get a bearing on it, leave it
close to starboard and then pass down the channel inside the Italian island
of Capraia, Elba-bound. In fact, one can theoretically remain on exactly
the same course the whole way down to the south of Capraia before altering
to port to make Porto Ferraio.

1. Villefranche to Naples

The wind, which had been light southerly all afternoon, later became
westerly, which gave us an uncomfortable motion on our course of 116
magnetic, despite steadying sails. For the first time for three years I was
sea-sick. At about 0200, Giraglia light came up and, once inside the shelter
of Corsica, we got some lee and later on the wind dropped to nothing, so

that dawn saw us ploughing through a mirror-like calm inside Capraia.

Before midday we were made fast stern-on to the bustling and hospitable quayside at Porto Ferraio (Iron Harbour), the principal port of Elba. Porto Ferraio is an excellent harbour for wintering in the Mediterranean. It is cheaper than the Riviera and there is relatively less dishonesty than in the Italian mainland ports, where conditions are often most unsatisfactory for visiting yachtsmen. The people of the island are charming, the harbour facilities are excellent and there is complete protection from weather. Small wonder that it is becoming a popular place to winter.

In sharp contrast to the previous weeks, the weather stayed kind to us all the way down the western Italian coast. The passage from Porto Ferraio to the newly discovered tourist paradise of Giglio Island was a delight. Sun, calm and reasonable visibility made a perfect trip. One passes at first close inshore along the northern coast of Elba, the rugged barren volcanic shores, interspersed with green valleys, making an unforgettable sight. If time permits, one can stop at Porto Azurro, the second port of the island, where there is also good shelter, or anchor off for a swim in the crystal water.

The tiny harbour at the island of Giglio (which means 'The Lily') had been enlarged and there was much more room to berth on the port hand on entry, where there was about 3 fathoms of water. The mailboat berths at a special central quay and the whole of the southern jetty was thus available for yachts. If you didn't draw more than a fathom, it was also safe to berth to starboard on entering, but here the protection was not so good. There was one road, one taxi and one superb view from the 1,000-ft-high citadel, built by the Dukes of Tuscany to repress piracy in the archipelago. Yachts are going increasingly to Giglio and two new hotels have been built.

An early start from Giglio made it possible to spend a few hours at anchor off the curious islet of Gianuttri, full of Roman remains on its hilltops and with Roman bricks still lining the harbour walls at Cala Mæstra, where the only houses exist. I had a look at this picturesque inlet, but there was enough northerly wind to make anchorage difficult (in any case, it involves a line ashore), so we made off around the south-eastern edge of the islet and found anchorage in Spalmatoi Bay, where two other yachts had had the same idea. Three hours are plenty in which to visit the island and after lunch we were able to weigh and set course across to the mainland at Civitavecchia.

Civitavecchia was once a pretty place, but war damage was considerable and there is now very little indeed to see. Many yachts use the harbour, however, since it offers good protection from all weather and—for some reason that I have never been able to fathom—it is about the only Italian port where one can be absolutely certain of getting duty-free fuel. One can, of course, get diesel fuel at ordinary inland prices ('prezzo nazionale') everywhere without trouble. But this price is very high—the cost of duty-free fuel ('prezzo estero') is about a quarter of the duty-paid, so naturally one makes an effort.

As in most Continental countries, however, there is a way around things. For, by declaring you are sailing for 'foreign', the Italian regulations allow of the issue of duty-free fuel. It is, therefore, quite astonishing how many yachts fuelling in Italy are apparently going to France. If you are not disposed to cheat, the agent fixing the fuel will be only too glad to cheat for you. The only snag is that, if the local Customs are out to do in yachtsmen, they are apt to confiscate your Customs papers ('Costituto in Arrivo per il Naviglio da Diporto'), so that you arrive at the next Italian port without papers to show where you have come from. I have never heard of this actually happening to anyone, as everyone stoutly resists such a confiscation, but it could presumably lead to awkward questions.

Civitavecchia was pleasant and helpful as ever. The run down the coast next day was made close inshore to take advantage of the lee it offered. The southward run is most entertaining and all the objects ashore can be distinguished easily with the aid of the *Mediterranean Pilot*. It is almost like a motor tour: one can go close inshore almost everywhere and, apart from the odd sand-bank, there are no dangers.

On passage we spoke to Civitavecchia radio station to ask for a met. forecast. They called us back after a few minutes and read out in Italian a long list of places giving present weather. This, of course, was absolutely useless. It is, in fact, regrettable that it is virtually impossible for a yacht to get a met. forecast in Italy. It must be humiliating for Italian harbour offices—as I have often known them do—to advise their questioners to do the same as they do and try to get the Malta forecasts.

Anzio—never a really good port—was chock-a-bloc with yachts whose owners were at near-by Rome at the Olympic Games. What in Italy, however, constitutes 'chock-a-bloc' would in France be considered roomy. Whereas the French squeeze in wherever there is room, the Italian harbour masters insist on several feet from boat to boat. It took me nearly 2 hours to persuade the Anzio harbour office that there was heaps of room for us, if only they would move a big Portuguese ketch a few feet one way. It was 'impossible' for a very long time: it quickly became possible when the usual methods of persuasion were displayed. Diesel fuel was also available here at lira 23 per litre (a most reasonable price), but the Customs took so long coming that we finally sailed next morning without it.

Southwards from Anzio, one has the choice of coasting towards Naples, possibly putting in at Gaeta, or taking the island route via Ponza, Ventotene and Ischia. The latter is far the more interesting passage, so we set off for Ponza, the only inhabited one of the Pontine Islands, 62 miles from Anzio on a south-easterly course.

The first thing you see on sailing from Anzio is usually the peak of Cape Circeo away to port. At first this looks like an island and one could imagine it to be one of the Pontine group, but as one gets farther seaward the low land joining it to the mountains inshore becomes clearer. Ulysses was here. At about that moment the three main Pontine Islands usually show up and one should set a course for the centre of the passage between Zannone (to port) and Ponza. Having made the middle of this channel, you turn 90 degrees to starboard and this new course leads you right into the harbour mouth of Ponza itself. The town—indeed the whole island—is utterly charming. The people are kindly and simple and the harbour authorities are very helpful to visitors. All yachtsmen who go there want to return. Among the 'sights' are some sinister half-submerged caves where, in the days of Imperial Rome, fierce eels were kept. To improve their gastronomic qualities, live slaves used to be fed to them. The harbour is well protected from all winds except those from the south-east.

Most yachtsmen steering south from Ponza take the direct route to Ischia. This is a pity, for in doing so they fail to visit Ventotene, an islet of lava which is seldom visited, but which is unique in the possession of its original Roman harbour hewn out of the solid rock. We were determined not to miss the curious spectacle and went to some pains, circumnavigating the oddly shaped lava coastline and finally, with some difficulty due to swell, making the narrow harbour entrance. I would not recommend anyone drawing over 6 ft to use this harbour and on the first occasion he should take one of the many pilots that present themselves to make quite sure. In heavy weather the entry would be impossible to all except local craft. The island itself has little to offer: we walked up into the village, where formerly political refugees were imprisoned, and visited some of the lava cliffs and creeks, the stone worn into a thousand shapes by weather over the years. One day suffices.

On a southerly course from Ventotene one passes close to the tiny islet of San Stefano, on which we saw an imposing fortress prison. The few slopes of soil were covered in vineyards, where we imagined the prisoners were allowed to exercise. We were told that only the really bad boys were sent here.

It was not long before Ischia showed up ahead and the same evening saw us entering the narrow approaches to the flooded volcanic crater that is the harbour of Porto d'Ischia. Many yachts of all nationalities were berthed stern to the ample quays. It is always a delight to be in Ischia. Apart from the harbour being superbly protected, the facilities for wintering and repairs are excellent.

And so it remained only to carry on next day to Naples, a matter of a couple of hours' cruising. There is always some doubt in Naples where to berth. I have been in all three harbours—the large commercial harbour, Santa Lucia and Mergellina. Of the three, assuming you have an average-sized yacht, I unhesitatingly recommend Santa Lucia. The commercial harbour has obvious disadvantages of dirt and uncertainty, the Mergellina harbour is too far from the centre of the town and the construction of the quays, necessitating ridiculously long stern gangways and lines, leaves a great deal to be desired. True that Santa Lucia, where one puts one's stern to a quay full of restaurants and cafés, is a noisy place of an evening. But you are right in the middle of things, the restaurants will give you fresh water (albeit at a grotesque price), the fuel companies will send you fuel and the ship chandlers will be glad to visit you.

No visit to the Bay of Naples is complete without including Capri. And so, after a brief lunch-time visit to friends at La Gaiola (an islet north of Naples) we found ourselves edging nervously into the somewhat inadequate harbour of Marina Grande at Capri. I say inadequate, since this small harbour is grossly overloaded all the season with ferries from Naples and Sorrento. A yacht therefore gets a very thin time of it: in fact, no yacht is in the season allowed to remain in the port between 0900 and 1900, unless she is lucky enough to get one of the coveted berths immediately to starboard on entering. Her only course, therefore, is either to anchor off Marina Grande harbour (where there is almost always a swell) or to go around the other side of Capri, where Gracie Fields's bathing-pool is the great attraction, and again anchor.

Here the swell is almost worse. In fact, I cannot honestly recommend a visit to Capri in a private yacht. It is a delectable place—albeit an out-and-out tourist trap—but the way to see it is from a ferry from Naples and perhaps a night ashore in one of the myriad 'pensiones'. Avoid yachting to Capri.

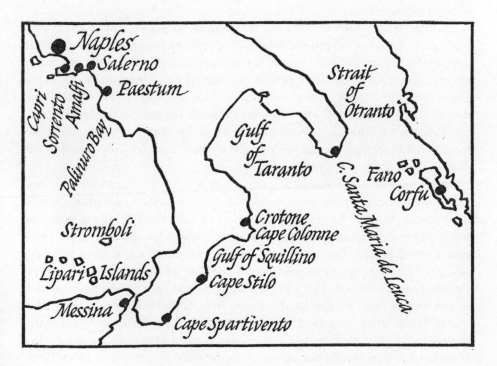

2. *Italy—'Around the Heel and Toe'*

The trip along the glorious coastline to Amalfi, however, more than outweighed the irritations and discomforts of Capri. We went close inshore all the way—one can even pass inside the little Galli Islands—and made Amalfi at dusk. I would have liked to stop at Positano, about which one hears so much these days, but there was no harbour there and we did not want to risk a night at anchor in a swell again.

The amenities of the small harbour at Amalfi were in sharp contrast to the beauties of the coastline. The harbour is not well protected at all, even from the prevailing southerlies, and we were very lucky indeed that the night turned out to be flat calm, or things would have been most unpleasant. The town itself is, of course, enchanting and of especial interest to seafarers. It was from this miniature republic in medieval times that the code of maritime law accepted throughout the world sprang in the form of the celebrated 'Tables of Amalfi', priceless documents which can be seen at the local museum.

Having 'done' Amalfi, we were relieved to be able to make the 9-mile passage to Salerno, where we found an excellent harbour sheltered from all weather. The harbour master's staff were unusually kind and made arrangements for us to hire a taxi to visit the spectacular ruins of Paestum, about 15 miles away along the coast. This ancient Greek settlement, dedicated to the sea-god Poseidon, was a great seaport at the height of its fame, but is now mostly several miles inland. Its many temples, however, still form a landmark to mariners in the vicinity and are mentioned in the *Mediterranean Pilot*.

From Salerno southwards, a yachtsman is more hard put to it to find suitable harbours, which are few and far between. After consultation with the harbour master, however, we decided to take the 7-hour leg next day to a place called Palinuro Bay, of which we heard for the first time. I was glad to read in the *Pilot* that it was an excellent anchorage, even in heavy weather. We found there was no actual harbour at Palinuro Bay, nor even a mole, but we anchored in good holding-ground and went ashore to look at the village and at the local French-run 'Club Mediterranée', which consisted of some hundred Tahiti-style thatched huts and a central restaurant. I suppose it is the French equivalent of a holiday camp. We noticed that free small-boat sailing was included in its many attractions, not the least of which was a flock of very forthcoming hostesses.

Palinuro Bay, which we left next morning at dawn, proved an excellent jumping-off point for Stromboli, the island I had meant to visit ever since, as a small boy leaning over the rail of the P. & O. ship coming from Australia, I had been much impressed by its blazing cone. It was perfect weather—sunny and a flat calm—and I see from my log that we first sighted this extraordinary island at 1030, some 4 hours after sailing.

Approached from the north-east, Stromboli makes an eerie impression. It is eternally topped with its own sulphurous smoke and a gentle stream of lava, interspersed with the odd molten boulder or two, trickles slowly down its western slope. It is dangerous to approach it from the westward, but the landing place and main settlement are to the north and north-east of the island. There is no lighthouse, but a light is exhibited on a rocky islet known as Strombolicchio, a mile or two to the northward.

My echo-sounder showed great depths until very close inshore and I, for a while, thought a landing would be impossible, but at length a fisherman came out and indicated a safe anchorage near the black lava beach. We rowed ashore and had a lobster meal, resisting all temptations to take a guide up to the crater. Conversation was mostly about eruptions: I gathered that almost everyone had already left the island and that the attempts to make it a tourist centre had failed dismally. At midnight we rowed back aboard. There was a curiously malignant atmosphere about everything, but we would not have missed it for worlds. I suppose we were about the only yacht ever to have spent the night there.

After a night of almost unendurable rolling, we gladly weighed for Messina. I half had it in mind to visit some of the other Lipari Islands (of which Stromboli is one), but the knowledge that none of them boasted a proper harbour determined us to give them a miss. There is quite a strong tidal run through the Strait of Messina, caused partly by the usual factors determining tides and also partly by the difference in salinity between the Tyrrhenian Sea (to the north) and the Ionian Sea. I had calculated the slack as at $4\frac{1}{2}$ hours after H.W. Gibraltar, after which a south-going current in the Strait would be encountered, favouring us on passage to Messina. These currents are locally known as 'Scandente' (south-going) and 'Montante' (north-going). We duly arrived as the 'Scandente' set in and the dreaded whirlpool of Charybdis presented no terrors. In fact, it is never a terror these days, though some believe that before the several earthquakes in medieval times, when the sea-bed was differently shaped, it was much more of a menace than today. As for Scylla, the other danger feared by the ancients which we saw vaguely over to port, it was nothing more than a bit of rock. We had seen much worse in Brittany.

Messina is not a harbour I can recommend to a yacht. On the chart it looks good. But the immense amount of railway ferry traffic between it and the Italian mainland involves endless swell in the harbour, and this is allied to some considerable noise.

Its solitary attraction to a yachtsman is that, for some inexplicable reason, one can fuel here duty-free without any of the troubles you get in Naples. In fact, one has difficulty in beating off the many 'agents' and others who want to fill you up. Fresh water—which we found to be heavily chlorinated—was available by paying the absurd price of 1,000 lire (about 12s. 6d.) for it. I afterwards learned that the official price was 90 lire per ton. The British Consul was a tower of strength.

Messina proved so distasteful that we decided to sail in the afternoon of the day after our arrival. It had been raining, but the winds had dropped, and while still in the Strait I had a R/T chat with Radio Messina, who told me we were in for a quiet night. This was the nearest approach to a proper met. report that I have ever had in Italian waters. It was a welcome change to be at sea on this starry calm night. Navigation from light to light close inshore as we rounded the 'toe' of Italy was easy. Soon after ten o'clock we were off the celebrated Cape Spartivento and set course for the next light, on Cape Stilo, which we made at 0330 and set course 078 degrees across the Gulf of Squillino. Many yachtsmen have complained of the lack of ports of refuge along this stretch of the Italian coast and I can quite see that this is a well-founded complaint. With a northerly wind, there is heaps of shelter close inshore and coasters even discharge into lighters at various points, but with southerlies it is quite another thing and you must be sure of your weather before making these long passages.

But the sea all that night was kind. It was not until about 0930, as we were making Cape Colonne (there is a ruined temple on it) at the approaches to Crotone, that it suddenly blew up from the west and the low sandy shore was blotted out. It was a typically Mediterranean freak.

We made Crotone—the only port between the 'heel' and 'toe'—for lunch. I had spoken to the agent there on the R/T earlier and he had dutifully laid on fuel, water and provisions. This is an excellent place for a yacht to take on duty-free fuel, as she can quite legitimately claim to be going foreign to a Greek port and the authorities are only too glad to help. The town itself is of no interest. I forgot to mention that at first light that morning we had found our quarter-deck all covered with dead flying-fish. Can one eat these?

Although Crotone is hardly a sightseer's paradise, the people were charming. The agent worked like a fiend for almost no reward and we even had a visit from the operator at the Crotone R/T station to whom we had spoken. When I came aboard late that evening, I found he had left a note in English (?): 'Plis theen oclok my spik for you Radio 2182. Remember. Goud naith. Saluti. Crotone Radio.'

He was as good as his word and at 1000 next morning we were again interchanging rather laboured greetings in Anglo-Italian with Crotone. The passage across the Gulf of Taranto was enlivened by a Force 4 following breeze, which made us set the sails and we charged along toward the 'heel' at a rate of knots. I had arranged for our mail to be sent Poste Restante to the tiny Italian town of Santa Maria de Leuca—right on the 'heel'—also some charts, so we decided to make it for the night, although the *Pilot* was not exactly encouraging and there were no lights to come in on. There is usually a south-going current of about 1½ knots in this area, coming out of the Adriatic, and we found we had not made enough allowance for it, so that Santa Maria turned up too far over to port, but we eventually made the inside of the mole in the dark after many misgivings, shared by the inhabitants, who clustered on the edge of the quay shouting directions. There is very little water in most of the harbour. There are no leading or other harbour lights, as the Italian authorities do not want the port to be recognized or used more than is necessary. But I learned that in the season quite a few yachts of various nationalities do make an overnight stop here.

Anyway, it was good to have arrived. I collected the mail from the post office successfully and we put out an anchor amidships to hold us off the quayside in case a swell should develop. We later learned that this was standard practice in ports in this part of the world.

After a day of small repairs in Santa Maria, we slipped at 0900 on October 2 for Greece. It was a thrilling feeling to be about to visit an entirely new country. Weather was perfect (lucky, because the Otranto

Channel has a bad reputation) and the Greek island of Fano (sometimes called Othonoi), where I was planning to spend the night, was plainly visible soon after sailing. A little later the Albanian hills came into sight. I would have liked to avoid the night at Fano and carry straight on to Corfu via the notorious Corfu North Channel, but we had heard such unpleasant things about the Albanians and their savage ways that we decided not to attempt this narrow international channel at night.

As we rounded the south-western cape of Fano, the so-called harbour mentioned in the *Pilot* hove into view. I could see some small shipping in it, but there were a number of reefs, with the seas breaking on them, just outside it, so we stopped and hoisted 'G'. A couple of Greeks in a boat came alongside and indicated by gestures that the harbour was impracticable. They boarded us and piloted me to an anchorage in a relatively sheltered bay. Later, we went ashore to look at the harbour, but its maximum depth was only 3 ft 6 in. and the approach was hideously dangerous, so we were glad to be where we were. Our first night on Greek soil saw us being entertained to beakers of *ouzo* (a sort of aniseed drink) and curious-tasting local fish by the local policeman. We felt tremendously at home and very glad that we had come.

Dawn saw us weighing and setting course for the northern tip of Corfu Island, where its hills seemed to merge with those opposite in Albania. The Corfu North Channel lay ahead. We had been warned to hug the Greek shore and this we did religiously. At one point we were within a mile of the Albanian coast and the houses could clearly be seen, but there were no Greek coasters close into their shore. Navigation was not complicated: the only spot where it seemed at all tricky was at the narrows near Serpa Rock, where the rock buoy has to be approached and left close to starboard. But from here we set course direct into Corfu harbour, which could be clearly seen in the distance. By 1100 we were fast.

Corfu is one of the nicest places I have ever visited. True, the harbour is not all that it might be when the wind blows northerly; when I first visited it in 1960 there was no proper fresh-water supply for yachts; fuelling was hilariously primitive; the food was strictly Greek; and the price of taxis outrageous. But never mind. The charm and friendliness of the Greek people, the fantastic beauty of their island, make Corfu the last paradise.

Clearing Customs on arrival was not easy, as nobody spoke anything but Greek. Two or three gentlemen describing themselves as 'Cook's agents', however, arrived, and with an unexpected fluency of English and

3. The Southern Adriatic

Italian quickly sorted things out for us. The quay at Corfu was lined with 'agencies' of one kind or another and we never quite made out who did what, but daily visits from 'George' and 'Apostle', who appeared to be vaguely associated with each other, helped to make life much easier. (*Note:* Since then—proper fuelling and watering facilities have been installed at a yacht station.)

We fuelled with much mirth from drums which were brought down on a cart drawn by a donkey. Whenever the donkey moved the cart lurched forward and the drums, which had to be piled on each other for reasons of gravity, threatened to collapse in a heap, until at last someone had the bright idea of unhitching the donkey. No one could find a pump of any kind. At last, fed up with the delays and unable to make anyone do what I wanted, I walked off to return an hour later to find that the fuel was being poured from a can all over the deck near the intake. In this way we managed to get a small proportion of the fuel we had ordered and several gentlemen later got hours of paid labour scrubbing our decks. It was a truly *Never on Sunday* atmosphere which everyone greatly enjoyed.

We were told that we would have to shift berth to water, but the man from an agency opposite let it be known that we could fit our hose to his tap, so that one was solved. Several people tried to get us to shift to another berth (just for fun), but we were able to resist this and stayed where we were throughout our week's stay in Corfu, enjoying every minute. We hired a taxi one day (at vast expense) and did a trip to Kaiser Wilhelm's palace and a beauty spot on the north-west coast called Paleo Castritsa (Old Castle). Then we hired motor-cycles (much cheaper).

The British Consul told me it was unwise to use the north channel in darkness. The Albanian fishing-fleet, he explained, often put to sea at night, escorted by gunboats which found it amusing to open fire at sight. We thought of making for the southern part of Yugoslavia on leaving Corfu. This would involve a long leg of about 160 miles up the Albanian coast. There are no British diplomatic relations with Albania (since the Corfu Channel incident) and so one cannot even ask for a visa. Some incautious yachtsmen, I learned, had actually been forced into Durazzo and Valona (Albanian ports) from points 20 miles offshore. Their treatment on arrival had been anything but kindly. It seems the Russians had a naval base with a number of submarines and coastal craft at Durazzo and they did not like to be visited.*

While based on Corfu, we made a two-day excursion to the neighbouring island of Paxos, some 30 miles to the southward. Other yachtsmen had told me that on no account must it be missed and I found their descriptions quite accurate. The principal village lies on the landward side of a mile-long sound, fully protected from all weathers. It is an ideal place for yachts: the authorities and people are delighted to see you. We entered by the northern end of the sound and sailed from the southern back to Corfu next day. Paxos is covered in olive plantations. We managed to thumb a lift from a builder's lorry to get orientated.

We finally sailed northwards from Corfu on October 9, passing through the Corfu north channel soon after first light and setting course for Brindisi, a distance of about 133 miles. The crossing was uneventful, except for the emergence of a considerable southerly swell. This is often found in the Otranto Channel when there has been a Sirocco (southerly wind) for any length of time. The sea seems to pile up here and can often be unpleasant. I was sorry to see the Albanian hills retreating into the haze astern, but realized this was the choice of the prudent mariner. We made Brindisi shortly before midnight and anchored in the outer harbour for the night. I had not got the necessary harbour chart to make the inner harbour at night, so thought it best to await the dawn. When I came on deck I saw that the shore signal station manned by the Italian Navy was asking us who we were. So we hoisted our distinguishing letters.

The inner harbour at Brindisi, which has existed from Roman times, affords excellent shelter from all weather. We bought a lot of foodstuffs, for we had no idea what it would be possible to get in Yugoslavia. Getting duty-free fuel was not nearly so easy. The local fuel merchant did his best to prevent us getting it: we could not think why. At length it dawned on us that he simply did not want to be bothered delivering such a small quantity as the 300 litres we had asked for. It was not until the harbour master intervened for us that the man eventually came to heel. The harbour office was very good to us, even going so far as to bring us along a real live met. forecast, culled, I saw, from Malta Radio. It seemed to us quite pathetic that the Italians had no reliable forecast of their own. Undaunted,

* Since then, of course, the Chinese have taken over!

I telephoned the local airport to ask what weather we might expect that night. They answered, 'Sail at once, for tomorrow it will not be so good. Tonight you will have light sou-westerlies.'

And so we sailed from Brindisi to Kotor, in southern Yugoslavia. It was the most unsatisfactory crossing I have ever made. We passed through Brindisi pierheads at 1615 and at once set course for Kotor heads on 105 magnetic. I anticipated sighting at least the loom of the big light of Kotor inlet about 0400, before first light, and Terry Hayes (my crew) and I went into watches after dinner with a feeling of confidence. During one of my tricks I noticed to my alarm that we were describing a circle. It seemed that our automatic pilot had altogether taken leave of its senses, for during the rest of the trip we had to watch the steering most carefully, with constant deviations observed.

The wind, which had been light north-easterly in the earlier part of the night, dropped and veered around to the south and later to the south-west from 0400 onwards. I was concerned at not sighting the powerful Kotor light, but at 0530 we did sight a number of lights which we at first thought were a fishing-fleet, but later to our horror turned out to be the lights of houses ashore. The failure of Kotor or any other light to turn up was most alarming and, realizing that our automatic steering had let us down for the first time in my experience, I had not even sufficient confidence to say for sure whether we were approaching the Yugoslav or the Albanian coast.

The wind had freshened considerably and rain squalls made visibility very poor. The jagged mountains on the coastline were only intermittently visible. Apart from the fact that we were some 5 or 6 miles offshore and presumably not too far from Kotor, we had not the faintest idea of our position. As we approached the coast the sea worsened, presumably from the reflection of the swell against the coastline.

At last we saw what we thought was the Kotor approach. It was almost impossible to read the Adriatic pilot due to the movement of the ship: to make things worse, the Serbo-Croat place names did not always correspond with those on the chart. I wondered if we would ever make anywhere. To our disgust, we suddenly realized that the heads we had sighted were not Kotor after all. We altered course and steered northwards along the coastline. No joy. For a reason I still cannot quite fathom, we put about and steered south, again coastwise.

Two hours later the miracle happened. We sighted a small harbour dead ahead, mercifully shielded by a long breakwater. We thought it must be Traste, a small place south of Kotor, but the size of the breakwater surprised us. At very long last we dropped the hook in the harbour: it was blowing Force 9/10 from the south-west and I felt lucky to have arrived anywhere—even if we were in Albania. A launch came alongside full of Customs and police. 'Where are we?' I asked in Italian. They must have thought we were joking, for they all smiled. 'Bar,' they answered. And so we were. Bar was a new port still under construction about 12 miles from the Albanian frontier. On the Admiralty chart, it was quite insignificant, for the recently built breakwater and other works were not marked. No matter, we had arrived.

The formalities were not arduous. We were at once granted the first two tourist visas ever issued in Bar—No. 1 and No. 2. We had to declare all the important things we carried aboard—cameras, typewriters, radio sets, fire-arms, binoculars and so on. No fuss about food, drink or cigarettes. Much less fuss than in England, in fact. Money had to be declared and written on our Customs pass, but I gathered it was just another formality. The official sterling-dinar rate was about 800, but tourists got 1,120 to their pound. The black market rate was about 2,000 to the pound and I gathered that most tourists arrived with suit-cases full of dinar notes and told every-one how cheap their visit was. We hadn't done any black-marketing, so we found life sometimes not very cheap. Since then the rate has been adjusted greatly in favour of sterling, and is now (1966) about Din. 3,500 to the pound.

And so we were well and truly in Yugoslavia. Modern Bar was a miser-able sort of place. I found a fellow who spoke English who arranged for some of our storm damage to be repaired on the spot by actually paying the workmen direct (an unheard of thing, apparently, and probably quite illegal). He said if we asked officially for it to be done it would take a month of Sundays and would cost us four times as much. I afterwards found this was only too true.

But Stari Bar (the old Turkish and Venetian town of Bar), now in ruins, was a sheer delight. One takes the bus and a guide shows you around with gestures and you afterwards take a 'slivovitz' in a café and talk animatedly in gestures, too. The hotels, we thought, were a disaster. The former villa of the King of Montenegro (we were in the republic of Montenegro, I gathered; one of the six that make up Yugoslavia) looked nice; it was now some sort of Party institution. As distinct from Italy, we were not once pestered by touts. This was a great relief.

The police wanted to know what our itinerary was to be up the coast. We had no idea. 'Tell us where we *cannot* go,' I remember pleading. 'Impossible. Where do you want to go?'—'I think I had better leave the itinerary to you. Make us out a nice interesting one.' And so they came back with a list of places to which we were allowed to go. This meant 'and to no other'. One did not *have* to go to all the places in one's itinerary, nor indeed in the order named, but it was an awful business getting new places added, so it was as well to get them all put in in the first place you called at. In fact, there were very few places prohibited to yachts; one of these was the island of Hvis, which was military terrain, and the other was Goli, a smaller island where people who disagreed with the régime were lodged at the Government's expense. In 1965 a new system of permits for visiting yachts—based on the Greek model—was introduced.

Two days weatherbound in Bar, then a rather dicey run up the dark coastline of Montenegro, the mountains frowning down on us. Kotor heads at last and the calm of the glorious fjord. The run up the inlet to Kotor is one of the most attractive things one can do in the Mediterranean and the ancient Venetian town of Kotor (Cattaro) at its head is worth going a long way to see. We tried to get permission to have some repairs done at the naval yard near by, but there was nothing doing. The Putnik (tourist bureau) man was very helpful. We dined ashore—better than I had expected. I would have liked a taxi drive over the sensational mountain road to Cetinje and back, but the price of £10 (not a very long drive) put us off. We found that at each port the Italian system was followed: we had to surrender the ship's papers and fetch them again before sailing.

The run back down the Kotor fjord and thence northward coastwise to Dubrovnik was happier. The sun shone, the sea was calm. The crew of a Yugoslav warship actually waved to us (this is not normal). The southerly approaches to Dubrovnik were like a beautiful dream. We entered the small harbour in the shadow of the battlements and made fast. I had some trouble finding an official. At length the harbour master arrived. 'You can't stay here. The only yacht we ever let stay near here was Mr Onassis's

Christina and then only because Churchill was aboard.' But he let us stay the night all the same, on condition that we went around to Gruz, the commercial harbour of Dubrovnik, next morning. It is a shame that they don't let yachts stay in the real Dubrovnik harbour, which is extraordinarily lovely, quite well protected and right in the middle of everything you have come to see.

Gruz, when we got to it next morning, was not at all beautiful and half an hour away from Dubrovnik in a tram. The tram ride was fun, but it became a little monotonous going backwards and forwards. I had an introduction to some Yugoslavs who still—to my amazement—lived in their prewar house, but when I telephoned them to invite them to lunch aboard, they politely excused themselves. 'It is difficult for us, you know.' In fact, the rule in Yugoslavia is that it is quite legal for a Yugoslav to board a foreign ship (including a yacht) whenever he wishes, but that he must get a permit if he stays aboard for more than 12 hours. This seems reasonable. In practice, only officials come aboard without demur.

Dubrovnik was one of the most intriguing towns I have ever visited. Its formation is quite unique and it is full of lovely things. The shops seemed better than elsewhere to date, but it was almost impossible to buy anything except the bare necessities, though there were heaps of these everywhere.

Though occasionally rough, the next leg up the coast to Korcula (on the island of the same name) was again one of great beauty, with the route following the inner leads most of the time. Here we spent two nights, interspersed with sight-seeing. The most friendly man in town was the Abbot of Korcula, but, of course, he was too afraid to come aboard.

At last the weather improved and we were able to leave for Split. There are two routes, of which the outer is the quicker but less sheltered. It took us through the channel outside Hvar Island and we were sorely tempted to stop the night at Hvar, which looked charming. But we pushed on, made a R/T call to Radio Split to give them our E.T.A. and found ourselves fast in Split at 1630 after a 9-hour passage.

Split is not a very good yacht harbour. We were in two minds where to go on arrival. Hard a-starboard on entering there was an obvious training-vessel made fast near an ominous hammer-and-sickle sign, but the berth looked too far away from the town. Over to port was what seemed to be a yacht club, but this also seemed somewhat remote from the centre. We afterwards learned that regulations in any case forbade foreign yachts from using the club's moorings. At last we found a small semi-sheltered basin just beside the harbour master's offices and put our stern to the quay there.

We were soon visited by the usual officials, including someone described as an 'agent'. Formalities were quickly over and I went to call on the British Consul, who seemed quite pleased to get a visit from a yacht. We were also invited around to one of the two local yacht clubs, called Labud (meaning The Swan), where we were most kindly entertained to drinks and dinner, and I was happy also to be able to ask some of its members aboard. I was not quite clear about the organization of yacht clubs in Yugoslavia, but it did seem that the members were, in fact, allowed to own their own small craft, of which I saw quite a number. There were, of course, no larger yachts.

We also got into touch with the Government ship chandlery called Brodokomerz, whose agents often came to see us during our week's stay in Split and were very helpful in getting us stores. I shipped several hundred litres of good-quality diesel oil at the duty-free price of 9 U.S. cents a litre. The arrangements for getting it aboard were, as in Greece, ridiculously primitive and a great deal of it got spilled on deck.

To our great joy, we were able to buy some duty-free whisky and gin, also some English cigarettes. Getting these stores involved some delay, as they had to get them sent down from Rijeka, where the State ship chandlers had their headquarters, but we had a day or two to spare, so it was not very serious. Normally, they will not supply cigarettes duty-free in Yugoslavia unless you take at least 10,000 at a time, but on this occasion we managed to persuade them to let us have 5,000.

There is quite a lot to see in Split, which is rather Italian in appearance and must have been a fine city in its hey-day. Most of the old town is enclosed in the ruins of the former palace of the Roman Emperor Diocletian, the Roman Catholic cathedral being built into the ruins of his mausoleum. The cellars have recently been excavated and are most interesting to archaeologists. As elsewhere, we found that all the necessities of life were freely available, though none of the luxuries. The restaurants were mediocre and not at all clean. The people, as everywhere in Yugoslavia, were very nice indeed. The harbour master and Customs people were helpful and even the police did not seem so crushingly negative as

we had heard from other yachtsmen. I had the impression that the Yugoslavs were trying to encourage yachtsmen to visit their country and were
being as nice as they could.

It was interesting to explore the possibilities of slipping and repairing in
Split. I visited the new Split Yacht Club, where there was a very good slip
which, I was told, would cost me $100 for four days' use (my boat is 54 ft
long and draws 5 ft), after which there would be a charge of $10 a day.
This corresponded roughly to what is charged in other Mediterranean
countries. I also had a quotation from a commercial shipyard, which was
much higher.

The greatest mistake we made in Split was to employ the 'agent' who
had been brought aboard the day we arrived. He was a very decent sort of
man and doubtless was doing what he thought was his normal duty, but
when I received his bill I saw that we had been charged about £25 simply
for his services, which amounted to next to nothing. In addition, we had
been charged about £5 for a very small amount of laundry done ashore
(we could have had it done for a quarter of the price if we had found someone privately). As the agency had done almost nothing and we felt we had
been more or less tricked into employing them, we felt somewhat aggrieved
that a small yacht was being asked to pay these fees. The reply was that, if
you used an agent at all you had to pay the minimum fee that any commercial vessel would pay—there was no special arrangement for yachts.
The agency admitted that many foreign yachts had complained, but none
had done anything about it. I did, however, and we got the British Consul
involved to such an extent that the bill was substantially reduced. The
moral is, 'never use an agent in Yugoslavia' unless you have settled in
advance what he is going to charge. I hope that as a result of these protests
later seasons will see a revision of the Yugoslav rules for agency fees for
yachts, because the small amount of currency thus gained does not compensate for the irritations and feelings of unfairness that it entails. It is
always a good thing if yachtsmen who feel they have a grievance will take
up the cudgels in self-defence, for only in this way will conditions for the
yachting fraternity throughout the world improve. It is no use sitting back
and suffering in silence.

The weather was not kind in Split and much of our visit was marred by
rough conditions in our basin, making sleep difficult. This was my fault for

being there so late in the season. It was already October 27 when we sailed, and many of our new friends came to see us off. I felt sorry not to be able to take them with us, as we slipped for Hvar Island that afternoon. Hvar is beautiful, has lovely buildings and the best climate (so we were assured) on the Dalmatian coast. Unfortunately, its harbour is not very well protected, so that, with the dreaded Sirocco freshening during the night, it seemed prudent next morning to slip and cross the straight to Palmizana Cove, where we lay at anchor for two days in a southerly gale, but perfectly happy and sheltered. Both the harbour master at Hvar and ourselves realized that our itinerary did not mention Palmizana as a permitted place, but as it was so very close to Hvar, they made an exception for us.

Our friends from the Labud Yacht Club at Split had given us an introduction to one of their members, known as Toto, who ran a small restaurant and *pension* on St Klement's Island, where Palmizana Cove lay. He turned out to be a great expert in skin-diving and we much enjoyed his company and that of his friends during our enforced stay.

When at last the weather improved I decided to take the inner leads passage southwards back to Korcula rather than risk the possible perils of the open sea. It was already pretty late in the season and everyone assured me that the stretch of the Dalmatian coast we had already visited (from Bar in the south to Split) was by far the most worth while, so we had decided to head southwards again. In Split, the British Consul had very kindly made inquiries through our Embassy in Belgrade about how we would be treated if we happened to call in at an Albanian port on passage south. There is an Albanian diplomatic mission in Belgrade that can presumably give this information. The answer had come back that—as there were no diplomatic relations between Great Britain and Albania—they could, of course, not give a visa or anything in writing, but that naturally 'any vessel of a foreign country seeking shelter in an Albanian port would be conceded the usual international facilities'.

I did not quite know what to make of this. After lengthy discussion with the Consul, we came to the conclusion that our chances of being well received if we made Valona or Durazzo were about 55–45, and then only if we could plead breakdown or weather as our excuse. Mere fatigue presumably would not be admitted. A glance at the international regulations, moreover, gives the impression that a vessel is only allowed 24 hours' respite in the case of bad weather. The Yugoslav yachtsmen that we met had stated categorically that we would be most unwise to risk it. And so we had decided against Albania, although we knew that this involved another Adriatic crossing back to Italy instead of a pleasant coastal run. I had therefore bought some good Yugoslav charts of the central Adriatic. These could not be bought in shops (no prize for guessing the reason), but were made available to us by the Yugoslav Hydrographic Service.

And so that evening, after a delightfully smooth inshore passage, we arrived in our old familiar berth at Korcula. I had thought of clearing for an Italian port from one of the outer islands, but was told that one must clear from somewhere where there was an authorized Customs post and Korcula seemed the most convenient. The wind had dropped, so we spent the night quietly in the exposed Old Harbour. It was nice to see old friends again and particularly pleasant next morning to run into an American family, Mr and Mrs Stanley Smith and their children and dog, aboard their yacht, a former Yugoslav sailing boat.

Customs could not clear us next morning as soon as we had wished, as their only representative was on the other end of the island clearing some Japanese fishing-boats, we were told, but this did not much matter, as we had the Smiths to talk to and the forenoon passed pleasantly. On being cleared at midday, which involved being given a piece of paper allowing us to leave Yugoslav waters, we rounded the southern tip of Korcula and set course from the lighthouse on Glavat Island, 190 miles across to Italy, where I expected to make the approaches to Bari early next morning.

I must confess we did not at all like the look of the weather in these early stages, so we called up first Split Radio on the R/T (no reply) and then Ancona Radio, some 200 miles distant. Ancona came through loud and clear and, although to our disgust they were quite unable to give us a forecast, they did to some extent reassure us by giving us present weather along the eastern Italian seaboard, which was more or less windless, so we continued on passage.

The wind freshened during the night and the rolling that motor boats so dislike started. We were about to alter course to avoid damage when the loom of the big light at Bari (visibility 21 miles) turned up and we decided to stick it out. I made my E.T.A. to Bari Radio as 0530 and it was at that moment that we entered Bari pierheads, just as first light was breaking.

There was a considerable south-going current offshore, just as the *Adriatic Pilot* had warned.

Bari is a big commercial harbour and a fine city. I had not been there before. We lay at the quayside inside the free port area, so that we were under police protection and control, involving showing of passes at the gate when we went ashore. This meant the blessing of a certain quiet night. I thought of shifting berth down to the yacht club in the middle of the town, but it seemed hardly worth it. All the officials, police, harbour master and Customs, were most co-operative. Bari is a port where you can get duty-free facilities for wines, spirits and tobacco. You can also get duty-free fuel, but, as usual, the local oil companies are not anxious to deliver in small quantities, as they feel the trouble is not worth while.

The coastal run down from Bari to Brindisi was a pleasant change after the bad weather we had recently been having. At first I had thought of making Otranto, 105 miles distant, but prudence seemed to call for an overnight stop with our old friends at Brindisi, for we had not got a large-scale chart of Otranto harbour and the entry looked a little difficult at night. We duly made Brindisi after a relaxing 9 hours' coastal run, with the low Italian east coast visible all the way. It was refreshing to be there without having to cadge for duty-free fuel again. Brindisi is a pleasant enough place, but no good to a sightseer. The only thing of interest is right on the quayside, a couple of ruined columns marking the end of the Appian Way.

Next morning we started early to make sure of getting to Otranto, our next point south, in the early afternoon. Once again, we had tied ourselves to this port by having our mail sent there in advance. I had chosen Otranto, knowing it to be the point of no return where we would finally have to make up our minds where we were to winter, Malta or Athens. A yachtsman in these waters has a wide choice of winter harbours, but there are many influences at work in his mind before he can reach a decision. Malta is from many points of view a sound choice: it is British, there are no currency troubles, Customs are probably kinder than they are elsewhere. There are excellent facilities and a labour force crying out for work. In addition, it only costs about £35 return to get there from the U.K. All these things are in its favour.

On the other hand, Malta is a long way from anywhere else one might want to visit next season. To get to it from the Adriatic in a small boat in November—even coasting—is a hazardous and probably lengthy business. Whereas—I reflected—at least we knew the Greeks to be good chaps: prices had not seemed absurdly high. The trip to Athens was more fun and not nearly so hazardous as that down to Malta. And then there was next season to consider. All these thoughts—and some others—passed through my mind as we ploughed the unruffled seas down the coast to Otranto. Meanwhile the glass was falling steadily.

At Otranto, we found ourselves in sole possession of the harbour, which seemed to be undergoing repairs. The entry was much easier than I had feared, but this did not prevent a couple of overzealous fishermen from coming alongside and boarding us as pilots. They had to be repelled with much mutual antagonism. During the ensuing night the storm broke and we were thankful for the protection of Otranto mole and its Angevin Castle on the other side. The small town of Otranto boasts its castle and a glorious small cathedral. Otherwise there is absolutely nothing—not even a bank to change money. It is the end of the world. It was already November 7 when the storm abated enough for us to put to sea, though there was a heavy southerly residual swell running. I went to the harbour master and cleared for Crotone, the next port towards Malta, though my subconscious mind told me we would never get there. Walking back to the quay, I at last knew my real mind. I took our passports out of the ship's safe, handed them in at the police station and had them stamped for leaving Italy. 'Where are you going?' said the inspector kindly. 'To Corfu,' I replied, 'and then to Athens.' He shrugged his shoulders. 'Take care when you go through the North Channel,' he muttered. 'Ships never use it at night.'

And so at midday on November 7, 1960, we edged carefully out of Otranto harbour and set course for Greece. There was still quite a swell in the redoubtable Otranto Channel coming up from southward and, with the sea on the beam, things were not very comfortable.

On course 108, we were aiming to pass between Fano and Merlera Islands before altering down into the Corfu North Channel. About an hour after sailing Fano Island did indeed show up and thenceforth proved a valuable seamark. The sea abated somewhat as we approached the Greek side of the Adriatic. I had at first meant to steer between Fano and Merlera to minimize the risk of night complications from any possible Albanian gunboats.

As dusk fell and the sea smoothed out, however, we plucked up courage and decided, in order to shorten the route, to steer north of Merlera, which we eventually passed within a cable or so of our starboard beam. The

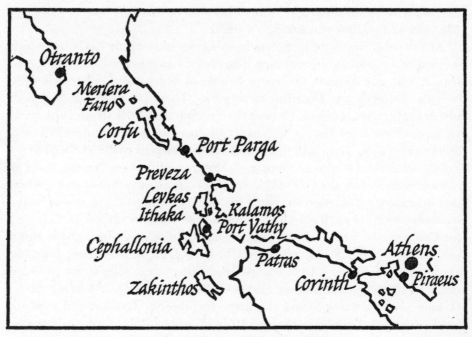

4. From 'The Heel of Italy' to Athens

Merlera light is very much less powerful than the big light on Fano, so it was some while before it came up, and the many lights on the Albanian shore at first caused us some confusion—not to say alarm. On leaving Merlera astern, conditions became perfect. There was bright moonlight and a flat calm. Had there been any shipping in sight, we could easily have spotted it. I left all our flags flying to indicate our intentions—just in case. At length the red light on the rock in the middle of the North Channel came up; we left it to port, swung to starboard at Serpa Rock light buoy in the narrowest part of the channel and Corfu with its myriad lights lay ahead of us. We dropped anchor off Corfu harbour at 0050 next morning, turned in and had a good sleep.

The Greeks were quick to notice the arrival of a foreign yacht flying 'Q' in their waters and early next morning we were boarded by a naval launch and instructed to enter harbour for clearance. It seemed even earlier than it was, since our watches had not yet been put forward an hour to comply with eastern European time, which is kept in Greece.

It was fun being in Corfu again. Everyone now was an old friend. The officer commanding the Corfu naval station asked us to dine and lent me the charts to get down to Athens. In Greece most charts used are the British Admiralty ones—a great compliment to us and evidence of the strong ties between the two countries at sea. They are expensive in Greece, so it is as well to bring one's own with one. The Commander—for so he was —told me that, in addition to being C.O. of the local naval base, he was also *ex officio* commodore of the local yacht club. He spoke of the efforts that he was making to get yachts to visit Corfu and of the improved facilities that were planned. It was intended, he added, to eliminate harbour dues for yachts as soon as the regulations could be changed.

After fuelling duty-free in Corfu, we slipped and steamed south once more. The C.O. had advised us to try spending the night at Port Parga, a small but beautiful cove on the mainland. On arrival, however, we found that there was too much incoming swell in the anchorage to make the night comfortable and I decided to weigh and set course farther south to Preveza, which looked like being a sheltered port. We were in two minds whether it might not have been more fun to enter the diminutive and ancient anchorage of Port Phaneri, close to Port Parga, but dusk had already arrived, the approach was not lit, and prudence once again prevailed. These little inlets—fascinating to every yachtsman—are all marked as plans on the relevant Admiralty chart.

Coasting down the Greek mainland at night with a slight following breeze in a calm sea and good visibility was delightful. The many excellent lights all duly showed up and the landfall buoy off Preveza was easily located. The channel into Preveza was easily navigated and we made fast alongside at 2215. The town is devoid of interest, but the harbour gives excellent protection. The Customs invited us to a drink on board a Dutch eel-carrying ship, the only one of its kind I had ever seen. She was spending the winter in these waters, collecting the eels that local fishermen brought her and shipping them back to Marseille—apparently a remunerative occupation.

Next day was a landmark—one that I shall never forget. In glorious autumn sunshine we coasted down to the natural channel that divides the craggy island of Levkas from the mainland, passed the silent, sunlit Venetian forts and found ourselves among the myriad Ionian Islands. With Levkas close astern, we had Kalamos to port and ahead of us lay fabled Ithaka, Kephallonia and, away in the distance, the flowered isle of Zakinthos. It was an unforgettable experience to pass into these historic waters where Ulysses had once sailed. Suddenly 3,000 years seemed as nothing.

We deliberately took the longest but most sheltered course through the islands, each more lovely than the last, the smaller ones often being un-inhabited and sometimes boasting just one lovely house. Many of these, I afterwards learned, were privately owned.

I felt like Ulysses himself when we finally made fast alongside the quay at Port Vathy, the principal township of Ithaka. The harbour master asked us to dinner (where else but in Greece would this happen?) and we took a taxi up the mountain to look at the spectacular views that once delighted Ulysses and Penelope. Everyone in Ithaka is a seaman; the boys all go to sea at an early age and return as old men, while the women, like Penelope, watch and wait. Ithaka is a magnificent anchorage.

Patras, a busy commercial port on the north of the Peloponnese, was our next port of call. It is not a specially interesting place for a yacht, but there are excellent facilities and, if you have the energy to make a taxi trip, historic places like Olympia abound.

As we left Patras to navigate the narrows on our eastward journey into the Gulf of Corinth, a fierce squall swept down the mountains to the north and for a moment I began to doubt the prudence of continuing. But another hour or so was to show us that even these fierce winds do not seriously disturb the tranquil land-locked waters of the Gulf of Corinth. In any case, the squall abated and we had a delightful passage along the classic North Peloponnesian shores.

I had determined not to pass through the Corinth Canal at night—that was an experience which I felt could be better enjoyed by day. So we were

at some pains to locate the tiny mole at the new city of Corinth. And here
for once the Admiralty chart let us down, for, instead of the fixed red light
marking the end of the quay which the chart showed, we found a flashing
green buoy marking the approach. These inaccuracies have since been put
right. A quiet night alongside ensued and in the morning the harbour
master sent a man to guide us to the ruins of Old Corinth, a taxi drive
away. These ruins are a 'must' for everyone.

From Corinth to Piraeus is only about 36 miles by sea, so we had plenty
of time to make this passage the same day. I swung out to face the western
entry to the Corinth Canal and saw the red flag flying that indicated 'entry
barred'. This soon gave way to blue, however, and we entered the world-
famous Corinth Canal. My echo-sounder showed a total depth of about
4 fathoms in the canal, whose sides are steep-to and high. We met no
traffic and were able to proceed throughout at about 5 knots. Passage
occupied 40 minutes. On arrival at the other end we were signalled to slow
down by a group of officials and a launch came out and boarded us. To my
irritation, we were asked to pay 20 dollars for our passage of the canal, the
minimum rate that a commercial vessel pays. I pointed out that we were
a minute yacht, but there was no budging them, and so, with rather bad
grace, we had to pay up. This sort of anachronism is productive of very
little revenue and produces bad feeling among yachtsmen and tourists. I
am quite sure that if the Greek authorities were aware of how the regulation
is being applied they would do something to modify it.

At 1700 we poked our nose into the Tourkolimanou Yacht Basin at
Piraeus. It was packed with yachts—some of them old friends—and we
had some trouble finding a berth. But the Royal Yacht Club of Greece
was most helpful. I was put into touch with an excellent agent for wintering the boat. And we were sorry to leave. Next spring, I reflected, I would
be back again.

2

Slow Boat to the Bosphorus

*Piraeus to Istanbul
and back a different way*

I have always wanted to take *September Tide* to Istanbul. I suppose it is the thought of seeing one's own Blue Ensign among domes and minarets, warding off 'baksheesh' seekers at boathook's length and proving to those Cassandras who warn one not to go just how easy it all is, that finally sets off the fuse to such a voyage. Anyway, I was in Piraeus, and Istanbul was only 500 sea-miles away. The temptation to go was something I could not resist.

Slowly, Poseidon's temple on Cape Sounion faded out of sight in the moonlight as my vessel rounded the headland and set course north. It was one of those many moments of decision that a yachtsman is always encountering: was I to steer north-east through the Andros/Euboea strait and so shape course direct for the Dardanelles, or should I take the way of the prudent mariner up inside Euboea, hug the northern Sporades, and so creep cautiously across to Turkey? There was not a breath of wind to mar the mirror of the night-time Aegean. But it was July, season of the dreaded Melteme, the whistling northerly that hurtles down from the high pressures of the Ukraine to fill the vast Near-Eastern depression, leaving scorched earth in the eastern Mediterranean. I judged it better to choose prudence.

One has to be careful in the Aegean; the 'wine-dark sea' of Homer is not like other seas. In summer, when one would most like to plough its salty waters and stretch one's limbs in the dry life-giving sun of Greece, the Aegean is at its worst. In July and August, says the *Aegean Pilot*, 'the north winds, known locally as the Melteme, blow with remarkable persistence'.

Remarkable indeed—a fresh to strong wind blows the whole summer (not only in July and August) night and day from June to October. There were, of course, occasional let-ups when hopes rose again, but these were usually short-lived—a day or two at most—and the Melteme would set in again, anywhere from NW. to NE.

The seas raised by the Melteme are short and very steep. Going into them a long and stout ship is not greatly inconvenienced; nor, indeed, is she even very greatly affected when they are on the beam. But the average yacht—especially the smaller motor yacht—is very seriously affected, and it is often dangerous to hold a certain course in bad weather. A sailing yacht by reason of her deeper draught and her liking for wind has a rather better time, though not much.

Another phenomenon of the Aegean is that one is virtually unable to obtain a normal lee when in the protection of an island. The Aegean islands are almost all thin and high, with the result that a strong wind blowing from one side of the island enlarges itself into furious squalls on the other side. Relative calm exists only very close inshore, where one would hesitate to navigate. The state of the sea, however, is often smoother on the lee side than on the weather side, so it is six of one to half a dozen of the other. Personally, in a motor yacht, I think it is wiser to take the lee side and exchange fresh winds and rough seas for strong winds and smoother seas. For a sailing yacht, on the other hand, it may well be wiser to stay on the weather side. All these things, and others, needed to be weighed.

Dawn saw us ploughing up the Khalkis channel. As usual, the best berth at Khalkis, where one almost always has to stop to await the opening of the swing bridge at slack water, was taken by a freighter, so we anchored off. The tide through the channel—a width of some 50 yards—is the most surprising in all the Mediterranean, attaining a rate of some 4 knots at springs. The swing bridge opens to allow traffic through only in the direction of the next tidal run at the slack preceding the direction of the tide. Sometimes it opens too late—due to railway traffic and so forth—and one is swept through at a rate of knots and often finds it a little tricky to make fast on the other side in a welter of unpredictable eddies.

Khalkis passed, we hugged the Euboean shore to starboard to minimize the effects of the Melteme, which abated during the afternoon. Euboea is lovely and unspoiled. As we approached the hamlet of Limni, about 6 hours out of Khalkis, I was delighted to recognize Sir Aymer Maxwell's Timmer-built motor yacht *Lady Delft*, and on dropping the hook gladly accepted the owner's invitation to go aboard.

After visiting *Lady Delft*, I pushed on to Aedipso, the harbour at Limni being virtually unprotected, and spent a quiet night among the Roman hot springs. On passage next day eastwards around the top of Euboea towards the northern Sporades, the weather became perfect. For once, there was no sign of the Melteme and, although I had planned to stop overnight in the anchorage at Skiathos, I decided, when I arrived at Skiathos Bay, that it would be foolish to stand up the prospect of settled weather and therefore pushed straight on around the north of Skopelos. Soon after dark I was able to make out the distant loom of the powerful light on the islet of Psathoura, most easterly of the northern Sporades group. Psathoura has an unenviable reputation as a place of wreckage. The treacherous south-west-going currents out of the Dardanelles sweep straight down on to it and it is surrounded by dangerous offshore rocks. Though excellent for fishing, the islet, which is only a few feet above sea-level and thus probably the flattest of all the Greek islands, can only be seen a few miles away and virtually not at all at night. So one thanks Providence for the tall and powerful light-house.

It was dawn when, in perfect conditions, we made Lemnos and were fast in Kastro harbour for breakfast. Though the population is entirely Greek, the atmosphere is Turkish. I was tempted to go sightseeing at the prehistoric cities in the north of the island and have a look at Mudros, the harbour famous as an Allied base in the First World War, but I thought it better to make use of this unprecedented spell of good weather to carry on to Turkey.

At first light we rounded the north coast of Lemnos towards the Dardanelles. It was a superb day and over to port could be seen the faint outline of Samothrace, with the Turkish island of Imbros plainly visible fine on our port bow. At all costs resist the temptation to land on Imbros, or indeed anywhere in this zone, which is military and prohibited to foreigners. In fact, the whole coastline from close to the Greek frontier right down to the head of the Hadramite Gulf opposite Lesbos is forbidden territory. Some yachting friends of mine were foolish enough to fish in the waters around Bozcaada Island one summer and were arrested for their pains—being forced to trudge for three miles wearing their rubber skin-diving suits in the blazing sun and I don't suppose they thought it very amusing at the time. The only really safe place to land is Çanakkale, at the Dardanelles Narrows, where one can be sure of being treated as a normal tourist.

A very odd thing happened about 10 miles out from the Dardanelles, when the landmarks could already be seen. What I at first thought was a tide rip appeared on the surface, extending across our horizon as far as we could see. On penetrating it, however, I realized that the strangely disturbed water was nothing more than the meeting of the west-going Black Sea current flowing through the Dardanelles into the waters of the Aegean. I felt we were at last really in Turkish waters.

The approach to the Dardanelles is to me unusually impressive. The Allied and the newly built Turkish war memorials are as conspicuous a landmark to navigators as the great lighthouse on the westerly tip of the European shore. Be sure to hug the European shore going east. At certain points the current is 4 knots adverse, but as one progresses towards Çanak-kale favourable eddies develop which partly compensate for the earlier delays. Avoid the middle and Asiatic side, where the currents are consistently adverse. I am told it is permitted to land at the diminutive jetty of Seddulbahir, just beneath the lighthouse, in order to visit the Allied cemeteries, but I think a permit from Çanakkale must first be obtained. One can sail within a few feet of the shore in very deep water and there are no offlying dangers.

Arrival at Çanakkale must be treated with care. The small harbour marked on the Admiralty chart is all right in theory, but there is nothing to show that a fierce eddy runs through it at certain periods or that the jetty is not a solid structure but merely a series of piles through which the eddies swirl unchecked. A night arrival can be tricky, as one may not notice the current and to one's amazement find the boat drifting helplessly broadside on into the piles beneath the jetty—as indeed has happened to friends of mine. The best course at all times is to anchor in the small protected bay immediately to the east of the port, which has good holding-ground despite the eddies, and there await the arrival of the Customs launch for clearance. Unlike some things in Turkey, clearance at Çanakkale is efficient and speedy, as there is considerable traffic in each direction, and the Turks are well organized to deal with it. Language is, of course, a snag, as the Turks usually speak Turkish only, so it is wise to engage a local agent who will clear you in and out for the reasonable sum of about £2. While at Çanak-kale it is best to remain at anchor in the clearance bay, although it is pos-sible to get permission to lie at a small pier which is usually reserved for official launches.

Çanakkale was filthy and smelly, but the Turks, most of whom seemed miserably poor, did their best to please. The rate of exchange was about 26 Turkish pounds for one sterling: the 'black market' rate was about 50 per cent more than this and we were glad that the regulations had allowed us to bring in some Turkish pounds we had bought in Greece.

We took an hour's taxi drive to Troy—well worth the experience, despite the appalling heat and the absence of guides. We also met some British officials in charge of the war graves on the other side of the strait. They kindly offered to show us around and I made a mental note of this opportunity for our next visit. Apart from these two excursions, the town offered nothing, although the surrounding country, most of it unfortunately in a forbidden military zone, was perfectly lovely and much more fertile-looking than in Greece.

One advantage of making Çanakkale was that the local agent managed to obtain for us a military permit to spend the night in the harbour of Gallipoli (called Gelibolu by the Turks) in the forbidden military zone in the Dardanelles. I was specially thankful for this, as there seemed to be no other port *en route* to Istanbul for miles.

It took about 5 hours to make Gallipoli, with an average 1½ knots of current against *September Tide*. Throughout, we stayed close to the shore, which was lovely, and reminded me of Devon and Somerset. There were no dangers. Before we berthed at Gallipoli an excited crowd of officials appeared and waved us away, but we went on doggedly and made fast amid a storm of protests. Five or six uniformed men jumped menacingly aboard, but the sight of my imposing document signed by the Governor at Çanakkale silenced them and we were shown to the best berth in town. It was clear, however, that we were regarded as strictly under escort, however friendly it might be. I could not shake off my captors all evening—even in the Turkish bath—and I ended up by despairingly giving a large dinner-party ashore for our guards, after which I was taken to an open-air cinema to witness my first Turkish film.

Getting away next morning took quite a time, as the official responsible had mislaid our *laissez-passer*. When at last we were allowed to leave—after the usual exchange of gifts—we were rewarded by a perfect day for motor boating. The Sea of Marmara was flat calm and the sun shone brightly from a cloudless heaven. As we made our way east, the currents of the Marmara became less and less. After an interesting coastal trip, we finally made the little bay of Erekli, 11 hours at an average of 7 knots from Gallipoli. Unlike all the other Turkish ports I had visited, there was absolutely no sign of an official: I afterwards realized that the Turks, having got you bottled up in the Sea of Marmara, wisely decided that, as you can't get out without formalities at one end or the other anyway, they needn't bother about you while you are hemmed inside it.

But dawn at Erekli was an unhappy affair. Gone was the cloudless blue sky of the previous day. A wild northerly was blowing and we were glad to slip as soon as possible. Only by hugging the shore from 0500 to 1400 were we at last able to make out the domes and minarets of Istanbul. The fabled city was ours at last.

It was pretty exciting to be at Istanbul. As we rounded the Seraglio Point very close to port, the whole city opened out before us. The current off Seraglio is fiercely west-going, and reaches $5\frac{1}{4}$ knots, but by staying very close inshore and following the practice of local craft, one can avoid nearly all of it. A far worse hazard were the numerous Turkish ferries—many of them British built—which flitted back and forth between one side of the Bosphorus and the other. We soon agreed with what other yachtsmen had told us, that it was absolutely useless to expect them to observe any courtesies, or indeed, the rule of the road at sea. You just have to be certain of keeping out of their way.

British yachtsmen we had met in Greece told us that the best place to berth was at a jetty off the Dolmabahce Palace, on the European side soon after rounding Seraglio Point and beyond the dirt and noise of the Galata commercial harbour. But we found to our disappointment that there was only a spot or two of water alongside the main quay and absolutely no bollards of any kind. Finally, despite eddies which went the opposite way to the main current, we got alongside the small jetty, where we spent a miserable night being banged against it each time a ferry crossed the Bosphorus. The surface of the water was filthy with diesel fuel, so our beautiful white sides suffered badly. I went ashore for dinner, and when I came back aboard I noticed that our deck-chairs had all disappeared from the quarter-deck and the table was half overboard. A visit to the police station produced absolutely no joy at all; next morning, however, an old man appeared and indicated by signs that he knew where the chairs were. Through an interpreter, he said that against payment of about 10*s*. I could get them back. I gladly submitted to this blackmail and he fetched them from a neighbouring ruin. It was clearly a put-up job: I later learned that it is quite normal for what the locals call 'water-pirates' to perpetrate this sort of trick on foreigners.

Istanbul is the most difficult place to get fresh water and fuel that I have ever known. Water is not laid on to any quay a yacht could use and one has to arrange for the State-owned water-boats to come and service one's vessel. This meant form-filling at my agent's office, a long wait, and then, when the water-boat did at last arrive, she was the size of a small liner, making it impossible to get alongside me at my berth. She had to anchor off and I slipped and pulled myself out to her. I later found that I had been charged for 6 tons of fresh water. As my capacity is exactly 1 ton, I felt this was going a bit far. Fuel was the same problem and my Shell Letter of Credit did nothing to help. After waiting all day for the result of the forms I had filled the previous day, a coastal tanker appeared, an endless wait ensued, and finally a hose was run over to us. The operation completed, I was told I must pay cash, that there were no duty-free facilities in Turkey for yachts, and that anyway the fuel supplied contained a high percentage of sulphur. I have since heard from other yachts that the yacht club at Moda on the Asiatic side can be of great use in getting fresh water, etc., and that one can lie there relatively undisturbed, though far from the 'sights'.

Weary and battered to bits by the wash from the ferries, frustrated to the *n*th degree by the delays and difficulties of fuelling and watering and distrustful of all men as thieves, I was glad to slip and sail Black Sea-wards up the Bosphorus. Our Consulate-General, the only really helpful people I found in Istanbul, had advised me either to go to Bebek, a sort of American colony a few miles east where there were mooring-buoys and some degree of quiet, or better still to a place called Therapia close to the

Black Sea end of the strait, where the British Embassy yacht *Four Winds* (a 27-ton twin Gardner-engined motor yacht) normally berthed.

In sharp contrast to Istanbul itself, the trip up the Bosphorus was altogether delightful. Local regulations require a vessel to keep to port when proceeding through the strait, as it so happens that the run of current is this way. In some places it is strong—up to 3–4 knots—but generally it is only about 1–2 knots. One thus sails eastwards along the European shore and westwards along the Asiatic. The main current, of course, is west-going and is caused by the excess of fresh water draining from rivers into the Black Sea being lighter than the saltier water from the Aegean. The local east-going currents are merely eddies caused by the contours of the Bosphorus.

The shore scenery was a *mélange* of Venice (at the water's edge) and Austrian castles (higher up) and was everywhere charming. The many mosques seemed to blend harmoniously into the almost Western landscape. We felt that this trip alone made our sufferings elsewhere in Turkey well worth while; local yachtsmen told us, indeed, that the Bosphorus area alone provided them with all they wanted, the only other excursion they took being out to the Prinkipo Islands just in the Sea of Marmara.

Arrived off Bebek, we noted a large patch of smooth undisturbed water inshore and outside the main channel, with the adjacent shallows marked by buoys. There were quite a few yachts at their moorings, mostly motor yachts, and the coastline seemed pleasant. The yachts, however, seemed a longish way from the shore and there were no visible quay facilities. We pressed on past the superbly placed Rumeli Castle, a medieval fortress which is one of the sights of Turkey and even gets floodlit at night, until the charming little bay and village of Therapia came into sight. The curative waters of Therapia were discovered in Roman times and the place gives its name to the word 'therapy'.

After Istanbul, Therapia was paradise. We quickly dropped an anchor and secured aft to a buoy with the aid of many willing boatmen, who were not of the 'baksheesh' type, had a drink to celebrate the advent of peace and quiet and went ashore in the dinghy to a curious but very edible meal at one of the several restaurants lining the cove, which give it quite a St Tropez atmosphere. *Four Winds* was moored close by and there were several other yachts to keep us company. By taking one of the communal taxis popular in Turkey and which wait to fill up with stray passengers before they start, we were within 20 minutes of the centre of Istanbul. I had a couple of swims, but the water, although clean below, was often covered with a thin film of diesel fuel. I gathered that this is usually so all over these parts.

A yacht visiting Istanbul is required to clear on arrival and departure, but any local trips she may make in the Bosphorus do not require clearance. The clearing-points are Istanbul itself or the last port before entering the Black Sea, a place called Buyukdere: anywhere in between, one can do as one likes. I therefore asked my agent in Istanbul to meet me there next morning and clear me out back into the Sea of Marmara. I duly anchored off my previous Istanbul berth, and the agent, with the police, Customs and harbour master came aboard to clear me. I was furious to find that I was charged $75 (£27) for agency fees and not at all mollified when it was explained to me that this was the minimum that, under a local agents' agreement, a vessel could be charged. To me, it was nothing but further evidence of how unprepared the Turks as a whole were for yachts generally. What with exorbitant fees for fuel and water, my total bill for the 5 days' stay in the Bosphorus came to over £50. I complained to the British Consulate-General, but of course it was too late; my advice to a yacht visiting Istanbul is to do nothing without first calling on our Consulate-General, where there is a naval office that is most helpful. The worst pitfalls may at least be partly avoided in this way, but one must remember all the time to be on guard.

I was not sure where we would spend the night on leaving the Bosphorus. I was in half a mind to call at the Prinkipo Islands, just outside the western approaches, or even at the yacht club at Moda, of which I had heard good reports, but I finally decided to profit from the current fair weather and try to get at least as far as Erekli, the bay where we had spent the night eastbound. And so, seething with indignation at the exorbitant agency fees and port dues at Istanbul, we set course westwards. With no adverse current—indeed perhaps some in our favour—we found ourselves off the entrance to Erekli Bay by late afternoon. I was in half a mind to enter it, but the *Pilot Book* spoke so encouragingly of the next possible port—a place called Tekir Dag, described as one of the principal ports of the Sea of Marmara—that I decided to push on and spend the night there. We duly made it at last light, but to my dismay I found that it was just the same sort of place as Çanakkale and so many of the Turkish ports. A jetty built on piles through which the swell surged unceasingly, a gaggle of coasters anchored offshore, these were the sights that greeted us. The night was far from quiet. Indeed, it is difficult to recommend a suitable port between Gallipoli and Istanbul on either side of this sea. If the prevailing northerlies are blowing, the anchorages—for they are little else—on the European sides of the Sea of Marmara may be used with prudence, but I am told there is next to nothing in the way of protection on the Asiatic side and even the few islands like Marmara Island itself offer almost no protection. A yacht with the speed or endurance would do well to make a direct passage from one end of the Marmara to the other.

It was a relief to leave Tekir Dag at first light and to arrive some 10 hours later back at Çanakkale, where, unlike Istanbul, the port and agency charges were quite moderate. I fixed with the Customs and Immigration, who by now treated us as old friends, to slip at first light, and we had a perfect trip with a 2–4-knot current sweeping us along down the Dardanelles out into the Aegean.

The Black Sea currents, in fact, swept us along with them all the way down the Turkish Aegean coastline, until, off Cape Baba, we finally waved good-bye to Turkish waters and made our approach to Mytilene (Lesbos). Although strictly Greek politically, this island still gives the impression of being 'Greece in Turkey'. It has considerable vegetation, several interesting remains and a friendly, welcoming population. There are two harbours— the northerly, which has slipways, but which is exposed and not to be recommended, and the southerly adjacent, which is well protected and has every facility. Mytilene is, in fact, an island full of excellent natural harbours and a yacht can spend a long time there exploring them. In sharp contrast to the dithering bureaucracy of clearance in Turkish ports, our arrival and documentation in Mytilene were the easiest things imaginable.

It was too good to last. After our happy calm, the Melteme returned in full force. Despairing of a direct passage across to the Greek mainland, I crept southabout Mytilene to give me as much northing as possible. The Greek caiques take this traditional route westwards. It thus finally became possible to steer 220 with the NNW. wind on the starboard quarter down on to the small and almost never-visited island of Psara, just west of Chios. There was a new breakwater here, of which the islanders, who spoke English to a man (again the result of a seafaring life) were inordinately proud. With Hydra and Spetsai, Psara was the main seat of the nineteenth-century rebellion against Turkish rule. Determined to stamp out insurrection, so the islanders told me, the Turks had razed the place to the ground, and the population, once up in the twenty thousands, was now but a few hundred. It was probably the most desolate and at the same time the most genuine Greek island I had ever visited.

In really rough weather we surprised the locals by sailing one morning for Andros and points west. We had some trouble making out the Kala-yeroi Rocks midway to Andros in the thick Melteme haze and the night in the vile harbour of Kastro in Andros was a nightmare of winds and anchors dragging. It took another 3 days of sheltering and anxious waiting and island-hopping to get back to Piraeus. But we had at last beaten the Melteme—and, more important, Istanbul was out of my system.

Let me give a warning about Turkish military areas. For practical yachting purposes, one can assume that the whole of the Turkish coastline from the Greek frontier to the head of the Hadramite Gulf (Edremit Koerfezi) including the offshore islands, is military terrain and you simply cannot land there. Yachtsmen who have done so have naturally been confronted with licentious soldiery and have suffered the inconveniences attendant on not bothering to find out things in advance. So the only advice I can give is 'Don't try'. In any case, it is doubtful whether there is anything worth seeing—even if you are a beastly spy. There are two exceptions: you can land at Çanakkale, as we did, and at a diminutive port beneath the Allied War Memorial, called Seddulbahir, to port on entering the Dardanelles. But here you must not visit anything except the memorials and cemeteries.

I can only describe our arrival (on another occasion) off Ayvalik (opposite Mytilene) as fully characteristic. Long before we had anchored or made fast we were boarded by a group of officials, none of whom could make themselves understood. I anchored in despair and went ashore, only to discover that we were expected to start the whole process again. The quay was unsuited for a prolonged stay and I got permission to go over to a romantically named village, where there was some lee, called Ali Bey. The place looked invitingly unkempt, but we were quite unable to enjoy it for the next 2 hours, during which the usual horde of officials milled around aboard, getting in each other's way, making scant progress with their business, but obviously enjoying it quite as much as we disliked it. After 12 hours at sea one is not always in the mood for an age of unintelligible formalities.

A soldier was posted at our gangway again—I cannot think why, except possibly to protect us from thieves, as we were no longer in a military area—and we sailed without incident at first light, weighed down by another sheaf of documents. No agent was available at Ayvalik or Ali Bey—so we were at least spared the expense of engaging one (they usually cost £2 or £3 a visit). I would not recommend other yachtsmen to visit this place—there is little to see, the formalities are infuriating and the neighbouring Greek island of Mytilene (Lesbos) is infinitely better geared to one's enjoyment. One lives and learns.*

The run down the Turkish coast southwards to Smyrna next day was enchanting. There were light following breezes, a cloudless sky and even the barren and somewhat repetitive coastline—we hardly saw a building or a human being—seemed full of allure. We even dropped the hook in a protected sandy bay and had a swim at lunch-time. Attractive as the adjacent desolation seemed, we decided it was wiser not to go ashore, though I dare say we could have done so with impunity.

Izmir (or Smyrna) is not a good yacht harbour, being fully commercial and not very clean. However, we were allowed to stay two nights in the old port alongside a water point, which proved a godsend, though it did take us an hour or two to have it opened. We were also able to fuel—though not at duty-free prices—and by agreeing to take a diesel fuel with a rather higher sulphur content than I normally use. The local Shell office, who spoke English, were unusually helpful, and again, one can only say that every individual Turk we met seemed anxious that we should enjoy ourselves. Even the Customs and other officials, with whom I spent the usual 2 hours clearing in and then out again—seemed keen to help and one of them who spoke a little English escorted me around the harbour from office to office as we gradually sorted out the maze of paper. It seemed

* Since then—things all over Turkey—with the possible exception of Istanbul—have greatly improved.

5. 'Slow

RIA

TURKEY in EUROPE

Therapia

Istanbul Bebek
Erckli Moda
Tekirdag Princes Islands
Sea of
Marmara

Samothrace - Gallipoli

Dardanelles
Imbros
Lemnos Seddulbahir Canakkale
Tenedos Troy
Mudros

Madramite gulf
Ayvalik
Mytilene Pergamum
(Lesbos) Mytilene Dikili

Skyros
Psara TURKEY in ASIA

Khios Iznir

Aegean Sea

Kastro Samos Ephesus
Andros Ikaria Kus Adasi

Patmos

Cyclades Naxos

Amorgos

Astipalaea

Santorini Rhodes

Castell-
Orizzo

Crete

osphorus

incredible that we could not, as in Greece and Italy and Yugoslavia, be given a manifest for use while clearing from one Turkish port to another, but apparently no such system existed. Footsore from my wanderings, I at last collected the various officials together—it was by then about 10 p.m.—and got them aboard for the final clearance ceremonies on the quarter-deck. They assured me that, had this not all been done the night before sailing, we would have had to spend a couple of hours preparing things at dawn—a time when I am not usually in the best of moods for filling in forms.

Izmir has little to offer on the surface, but we did discover an interesting covered bazaar quarter, where one felt one was really in the Middle East. The touts were a real menace, showing an embarrassingly extrovert attitude to tourists as they touted their various wares and services, often of an alarmingly personal nature. At the instance of the police, I hired a night-watchman who passed what I trust was a most comfortable night asleep at our gangway. I had not the heart to disturb him as we stepped over his prostrate form on returning aboard.

3
Return to the Wine-Dark Seas

*A winter in Malta
and back to Greece in the spring*

Ever curious, I conceived the idea, towards the end of that season, of wintering in Malta instead of again in Greece. This involved a trek westwards, but I felt it well worth while—if only for the pleasure of visiting Malta, which was new to me. I sailed *September Tide* up to Corfu—and back to Italy, and made Syracuse, in southern Sicily, my last port of departure.

The sun shone feebly for the first time for days and Sicily dropped astern. The sea was lighter in colour because we were in the so-called Malta Channel, where our course at no point lay across more than 75 fathoms. The Ionian which we had just left is often over 2,000 fathoms deep. I had last crossed the Malta Channel on a fine day earlier last year and had seen the difference in colour very sharply defined as the sea-bottom shelved upwards.

The land faded. The sea flattened. Shipping began to appear, mostly east- or west-bound through the Channel. At lunch-time I called Malta Radio and sent telegrams to the Queen's Harbour Master.

Around 4 o'clock in the afternoon land came up and soon afterwards the islands of Malta, Comino and Gozo were clearly seen. So far as I could tell, we were on course for Valletta, though I had not made the approach by sea before. Finally, some tall wireless masts came up, marking the port hand approaches to Valletta and I knew that all was well. Dusk was falling as we first made out the flash of the fairway buoy marking the approach to Grand Harbour, Valletta.

As we altered slowly round into Grand Harbour, there was a peal of thunder, a jagged fork of lightning and the heavens opened. I could hardly see through the rain to make fast. It was an arrival straight out of *Macbeth*.

As soon as we were alongside the deserted Customs House quay a man came running up to tell me that I could not stay there. He said he was a pilot. At the same time a boat came alongside with Customs and Immigration officers and told me to stay where I was. It seemed the only thing to do was to ignore both, so I put my stern close to the quay a little farther up the harbour and here we cleared Customs most pleasantly. The Maltese seemed very glad to see us and there was a letter from the Queen's Harbour Master about our permanent berth. The swell in the harbour was too great to allow a stern gangway, so we simply pulled ourselves in and jumped when we wanted to get ashore.

Next morning I had a visit from a Mr Podesta, of the Royal Malta Yacht Club, and two agencies, Sullivans and Ripards, left their cards. I could already see, from the oil on the water and the continued movement, that Grand Harbour was not a suitable place for a yacht, and so, collecting a scratch crew, I slipped out to sea for the newly building yacht marina around the promontory in the next harbour. This marina is at a place called Ta Xbiex (which means 'the place of nets' in the Maltese language). Where once the local fishermen mostly laid up their craft, it is at the head of Lazaretto Creek, which in turn forms part of Marsamxett, or Quarantine, Harbour. It was fortunate that the morning was flat calm, for there were many small boats moored in the approaches to our berth, but we managed to circumnavigate these and made fast to a buoy forward, with stern lines to the quay. The Customs had been most obliging about what remained of our duty-free stores: I was told that, so long as they did not go ashore, I could tranship them to our neighbour *Uhuru* for the winter. There was no nonsense about signing papers for the temporary import of a boat not registered in Malta, such as I have come across to my alarm when visiting English ports (the boat is registered in Jersey). And so we seemed to be fast for the winter.

I was delighted with our arrival in Malta. In most of the harbours we had visited in the Mediterranean we had become accustomed to long delays while we found out 'how to do it', 'whom to telephone' and even 'where to go'. Not so here. The other yachts made everything easy for us from the moment we arrived: there was an unusual spirit of co-operation. The

Maltese authorities were mostly evident by their absence, which is perhaps the best thing for authorities everywhere. But, as there was no further need for them, they were doubtless doing the right thing.

I was greatly impressed by the possibilities of the Malta yacht marina. There were facilities for fresh water (always a scarce commodity in these islands), fuel, electricity and telephones at the quayside. Other vital matters like refuse collection and a laundry were also there. Buoys were laid for mooring some twenty-five to thirty larger yachts stern to the quay. The Ta Xbiex Marina was, however, only a pilot project for a much larger scheme which some quarters would like to see put in hand as part of the general development of tourist facilities in Malta.

The island was indeed in a parlous condition in those days, with the Services pulling out and the Maltese cast on their own slender resources. Far the largest of these, there being no minerals, agriculture, industries or any of the normal attributes of an independently economic unit, must be the dockyards and the harbours, which were, after all, the whole *raison d'être* of Malta through the ages. I was, therefore, not surprised to learn that an ambitious scheme was in embryo for spending anything up to £50 million for developing the whole island as a sort of nautical base. This would apply not only to the harbours of Valletta, but also to the creeks and inlets throughout the Maltese group. Manoel Island, the centre of all this and abandoned by the Navy, would be a sort of yachtsman's paradise. Here, I suppose, ladies would be allowed to wear shorts and gentlemen to remove their shirts, both activities formerly frowned on by the locals. I hope I am alive to be present when this momentous scheme is finished. Meanwhile, the pilot marina at Ta Xbiex is a reality and will probably play an increasingly important part in Mediterranean yachting.

I was asked while in Malta to what extent yachts or yachtsmen based on the U.K. might make use of the two Maltese schemes. One can only reply that, as to the use of the existing yacht marina at Ta Xbiex, it certainly will be extensively patronized by British yachts wanting to winter in the Mediterranean, always provided that the costs are kept down. It must compete, not only with the more accessible French Riviera ports, but also with good wintering places like Ischia, Elba and the many Greek marinas now springing up. Malta has the supreme advantage that it is the best natural harbour in the Mediterranean and that its yards and slipways are unbeatable. Those in Manoel Island are the best I have ever seen for slipping and tending small craft. You could, moreover, get to and from London to Malta for as little as £33. 13*s*. and there was talk of reducing this fare. Duty-free stores are sold at genuinely duty-free prices (not the case in the other Mediterranean ports) and shopping for the sort of things a yachtsman wants is easy.

Geographically, of course, the island is not all that might be desired. Apart from the delightful islands of the group themselves, you have more or less got to go back to Sicily before you can get anywhere. There is no goal for a yachtsman on the inhospitable North African coast to the south, there is virtually nothing westwards unless you go 400 miles to Sardinia or 800 to the Balearics, while the nearest point in Greece is over 300 miles away.

I think, however, that these disadvantages might well be counterbalanced by the obvious advantages of being in Malta once you get there, always provided that the local people are far-sighted enough to keep costs down and give you what you want when you arrive. In view of the competition from other countries, this is frightfully important. Whatever way you look at it, and especially when you see how little is being done in the U.K. to provide facilities for yachts, the Maltese projects are not only very interesting but most praiseworthy, and I commend a visit to Malta to my fellow yachtsmen.

For those who do not care so much for life at close quarters with their neighbours, there are moorings in M'Sida Creek, not very far away. There seemed also to be possibilities off the yacht club and in Pieta Creek, but I was told these were not well protected. If you prefer to be surrounded by commercial craft in the centre of things, you could even go stern to the quay in the innermost recesses of The Marsa, but I think this berth might be unsuitable for those wanting to live aboard.

One of my most welcome callers while at Ta Xbiex was the secretary of the Royal Malta Yacht Club, George Lowell, who combined this vital function with the almost equally vital one of being Saccone and Speed's local representative. If you take on duty-free stores in Malta, you can stow them 3 days before actually sailing.

I had a last look at my boat before climbing into the aeroplane that took me back to London. She did not exactly look as though she had travelled nearly 4,000 sea-miles that season. Athens, the Peloponnese, that storm-ridden Aegean, the terrible Turks, Istanbul and the Sea of Marmara, Corfu, a touch of Italy, Sicily and now Malta—it all seemed a long way away. How strange to put on one's overcoat and be carrying a brief-case— almost like catching the 'eight-thirty-five' to London Bridge again. The aeroplane circled over Malta and gained height. Far below lay a slice of my life—but in safe keeping. For was not this, according to the Acts of the Apostles, the 'island called Melita . . . and the barbarians showed us no common kindness'.

Malta in April. First light while the city sleeps. The fresh still air tingles through our veins and sets us alight for another departure as we let go all and set course 034 for the bottom right-hand corner of Sicily. The season has begun.

I confess I am no hero. Yachting should be a pleasure and I like to minimize its risks and disasters—they come along often enough, whatever you do. And so, instead of taking the classic route to Greece direct from Malta to the island of Cephallonia (Hydrographer has even recently issued a special chart for this trip), I found myself relatively 'coasting' not too far from the shores of Sicily and the 'toe and heel' of Italy. The direct passage is nearly 400 miles (Malta–Cephallonia) and Malta–Corfu, the coasting route, is about the same, but with the advantage that you have several ports at hand should things go sour on you. Of course, there is the southward run from Corfu to Cephallonia to contend with later on, but that is a delightful trip in sheltered waters and need not be taken into account arithmetically.

By lunch-time *September Tide* was in Sicilian waters and, as the kettle came on to boil for tea, we were abeam of Syracuse, traditional port of call for yachts from Malta. Conditions, however seemed so good that I managed to resist the temptation to put into Syracuse (indeed a fair city) and continued on much the same course for the region of the Strait of Messina. As darkness fell, we could clearly make out volcanic Etna over to port, with the outline of Messina Strait ahead. Red lights circled everywhere in the heavens—aircraft and helicopters from the Italian naval base at Augusta. Helicopters add a new hazard to night-time yachting and I have heard of some mariners confusing them with ships' navigation lights—all part of the fun.

In the still of evening a troublesome short swell developed—the harbinger of the north winds that later struck us, funnelling through the Strait of Messina as we laboured on towards Cape Spartivento. Once inside the friendly cape, all was again calm and it was not until next morning, as we were fighting our way across the Gulf of Squillace, that once again the 'Maestrale' struck and I determined to enter Crotone. Until 1 o'clock that morning, we had been mystified by luminous explosions ashore: these were nothing but fireworks set off by the local villagers honouring their patron saint's feast-day unwittingly assuming the role of the medieval 'wreckers'!

Crotone is an awful place, but it is at least a harbour, and we were jolly glad to get in fuel, water and see to a few teething troubles. Everybody kept on asking for cigarettes—a tiresome habit in this part of the world. There is an excellent Shell fuel depot here and the agency is attentive. I had taken the trouble to fix an appointment with them by radio-telephone before arrival, so we got V.I.P. treatment.

A favourable 'met.' forecast from Malta Radio (the only reliable station in these parts) determined our departure at 1000 two days later and by dinner-time we were standing off the diminutive port of Santa Maria di Leuca, on the farthest heel of Italy. There seemed no need to break our passage, so we set course from the big light which here marks the southern entrance to the Adriatic over to the powerful light on Fano Island, our Greek landfall. The Otranto Channel is a nasty place sometimes for a small boat, but fate was kind and—with the Fano light turning up at 0100, we found ourselves entering the notorious Corfu North Channel by first light. We were in Corfu for breakfast and our trip around the Peloponnese could begin.

Corfu is a dreadful harbour for yachts. The authorities are always very nice and helpful, but the Yacht Station where one is generally supposed to lie is very exposed and suffers also from the usual effluents of a commercial harbour. The small perfectly protected harbour immediately beneath Corfu Castle is reserved exclusively for boats belonging to the Greek Royal Family (actually only used for a week or two in summer) and visitors simply have to lump it—an incredible situation in a major tourist centre. But I don't suppose anyone has had the nerve to suggest a change to the King, who would probably be the first to welcome it if an alternative port

Albania

Ionian Sea

Corfu

Igoumenitsa

Paxos

Ioannina

Preveza

Trikkala

Lefkas

Ithaca

Missolonghi

Cephalonia

Zante

Patras

Gulf of Corinth

Katakolon

Olympia

Nauplion

Pylos

Messini

Kalamata

Methoni

Sparta

Githion

C. Matapan

Kithira

6. Corfu to the Peloponnese

could be built for him. Gouvia Bay—rather half-heartedly suggested by the Greek authorities as an anchorage—is too far from things and not worth the trip anyway.

At Corfu we cleaned ourselves up, fuelled efficiently and set course for Paxos, the many enchanting islets surrounding Lefkas and arrived in the sheltered port of Zakinthos (Zante to the Italians) some 170 sea-miles later. It was here that our first contact with the Peloponnese was made. 'Zante, Zante, fior di Levante' goes the saying. We agreed. It was May and the whole lovely island was covered in wild flowers. Time has passed gently for its easy-going people. At evening, groups of young men parade the streets singing 'Cantata' to the girls at their windows or sit in the 'tavernas' making music into the small hours. In the country, people sleep on small wicker platforms built on stilts to keep cool. We took a taxi through all this beauty down to a bay where miniature Trinidadian pitch springs gushed out of the quiet green fields. Fortunately, the flow is not commercial. This bay, by the way, can be visited very prettily by yacht and we had a swim there next morning before pressing on to Katakolon.

On passage I had a chat on the R/T with the British yacht *Chinta* (John Crammond), who told me that she was experiencing fresh easterlies in the approaches to Patras, whereas we had a flat calm. These easterlies are a local wind often met with there at any time of year and caused by the configuration of the high land.

I cannot recommend anyone to visit Katakolon unless to take shelter or to visit Olympia from there. The port is depressingly commercial, but forms an excellent place to visit this very famous site, either by taxi if you are feeling rich or by the amusing local train if you are not.

From Katakolon down to Methoni the coastal run is 56 miles, so that a stop in the channel inside Proti Island for lunch breaks the journey pleasantly. We were, indeed, in some doubt whether to put into the little port of Pylos in Navarino Bay instead of Methoni for the night. I had been to Pylos before and loved it, but not Methoni, so we pushed on. Methoni looks very attractive from a distance, with its crenellated Venetian fort jutting out to form a natural breakwater, but the town is dead and the fortress is far better viewed from seaward than from ashore. I therefore strongly recommend a yacht to use Pylos rather than Methoni for the night. Pylos is superbly placed in the historic bay, dominated by a fine Turkish-cum-Venetian 'Kastro' gone Christian and the little town hums with life. Except for the ½-mile-wide southern entrance between majestic cliffs and a small unnavigable opening in the north, the great bay of Navarino is wholly enclosed and safe. In 1827 an Allied fleet defeated the Turks here and the final liberation of Greece followed. If you are a keen skin-diver you can still visit the remains of some of these ships, mouldering in the sandy bottom of Navarino with the memorials to the British, French and Russian sailors looking down on them. A couple of miles away are the ruins of Nestor's palace at Pylos, the scene nowadays of excavations by the American School in Athens.

As to the little port of Pylos itself, it is always alive and outward-looking, a sort of Clapham Junction for seamen awaiting a ship. There is usually a tanker in the bay opposite and several large ships might call each day for fuel. Big companies like the P. & O. use it as a regular place of call.

Leaving Methoni next morning, we were escorted out to sea by a school of dolphin leaping around our bows. The Greeks say that if you call to them in a special sort of voice, shouting 'Vassili!' (the Greek for the name 'Basil', meaning 'a king') they will stand up in the sea and turn round to see who is calling. Then if you shout 'Vassili!' a second time, one of them will dash towards you and join your ship. I have tried saying 'Vassili!' like this several times, but so far it seems I've not found the right tone of voice. Perhaps one day, when I am on watch alone and the moon is full . . .

There is also a Greek story about mermaids. If the sea is rough and your barque be in peril, a lovely mermaid will materialize. You must listen carefully, for she will call to you: 'Where is Alexander the Great?' Then you must answer with a great cry: 'Alexander lives and rules!' And the storm will be stilled and with it—alas!—the lady will disappear. I have often been in a rough Greek sea, but nary a mermaid yet.

Seamen in these parts lead special lives and have a 'lingua franca' of their own all the way from Italy to the Black Sea. Maybe the great maritime empire of Venice has left them this in trust. 'Laska! Laska!' you hear them shouting. This derives from 'Lascia', the Italian term, and means 'Pay out the line'. Again, we hear 'Founda!' meaning 'Let go the anchor' and 'Vira!' meaning 'Haul in'. 'Karina' is a keel, 'Albouro' a mast, 'Bastouni' a bowsprit, and so on.

While on this topic, one can also see a connection between the various Mediterranean tongues and the names of the winds the sailors know. Overleaf is a diagram of what they call the winds in these waters. You may make your own deductions.

There are several islets off Methoni and my craving for documentation led me to anchor at two of them—Sapienza and Skhiza—really just for the hell of it. Indeed, they do provide good shelter in their uneven coastlines, but that is about all, for from now onwards we were leaving the green pastures of the Ionian side of Greece and meeting the stern aridity of the Aegean. As we rounded Cape Gallo to enter the Gulf of Kalamata, we came upon a strange-looking craft stopped in a bay. She turned out to be a sponge-fishing boat. There was a collection of rather basic-looking sponges drying on her rigging and from her stern a diver was working, his air-line trailing over the side. There was an exchange of sponges for cigarettes and we went on through the channel inside Venetico Island.

There were several fishermen in the strait and we took the opportunity of trying to buy some fish. The price asked came as rather a surprise—some £3 for a few moderate-sized unspecified samples—so we found ourselves refusing. Fish in Greece is, in fact, a far greater luxury than meat, and some of the prices asked give one indigestion to follow.

7. The winds as the Greeks know them

After a pause to photograph the Venetian 'Kastro' of Koroni (but no good shelter in its harbour), we made Kalamata 3 hours later in a violent rainstorm. As usual, the official Yacht Station was blocked by a freighter, but we went to a better berth, where there was also fresh water, immediately opposite the shops and tavernas.

Kalamata is not a good yachting harbour. An attempt was made to charge me Dr.900 (about £11) for an hour's work on the port motor. After this had been successfully beaten off, the local Customs man refused to allow some Greek friends aboard for fear of smuggling. The place is divided into the port area, known as 'Paralia', and the upper town, which is more civilized and contains even some interesting Byzantine churches. A taxi-man between the two will ask Dr.50, but will accept Dr.20. For what I presume was a fair price of Dr.500 (about £6. 5s.) I hired a taxi for a superb road excursion to Mistra, a ruined Byzantine city extending over a whole hill-side near ancient Sparta (of which latter naught remains). The drive, often pretty hazardous, was of stupefying beauty over the Taygetus range and we voted it well worth the effort. To get to Mistra by road from almost anywhere is so difficult that few people ever try, so that it is one of the great advantages of a yachting call at Kalamata to be able to do so. Another excursion we contemplated from here was that to the Temple of Bassae, one of Greece's better-preserved temples, but we finally decided to leave this for another time. We reflected that, on the morrow, we were due to see for the first time one of the most extraordinary parts of Greece—never seen by the average tourist and thus a yachtsman's special preserve—the fabulous Mani.

The great day had arrived. We were going to see the Mani, the part of Greece that not even the Greeks know. During the forenoon we slipped from Kalamata in perfect weather and coasted down the eastern shores of the Gulf of Messinia to drop the hook off Kardhamili inside Chapel Island for lunch. I was thrilled that the sea was so calm, as I wanted to spend the night in the Bay of Limeni, from where we could visit Areopolis, 'capital' of the Mani, next day. The slightest wind from west through to north makes this impossible, but the omens seemed good.

We duly made Limeni and put our stern to the small concrete quay (complete with Yacht Station, I observed) and passed a mercifully un-eventful night. The bay was incomparably lovely, high cliffs towering to the skies and sparklingly clear waters beneath us. Just a few abandoned villages ashore. We ordered a taxi the previous evening and it appeared after dark, its driver clamouring for payment, which we felt obliged to make although we did not use him. Next morning he came again and took us up the terrifying serpentine road that leads to Areopolis on top of the hill. It was market day, so the village was overflowing with pigs, sheep, lambs and their owners. We thought the drive so frightening that we walked downhill to the harbour again, called on the only two inhabited houses, and sailed away southwards. Looking at the Taygetus range that carves the Mani peninsula in two, it was difficult to see how anyone could ever live there. It was just rocks and stones and pebbles and then rocks again.

'The Mani', says the guide-book, 'is one of the most original regions of Greece, as much for its beautiful scenery as for the customs of its people.' I endorse this. This rather frightening bit of Europe extends from Kalamata in the north down to Cape Matapan, roughly following the ridge of the Taygetus mountains. The only part of Greece never to have been under foreign rule, its wild inhabitants descend from the ancient Spartans. Even the Turks gave up trying to subdue them and did not quarrel when their tribute was never paid. The Maniots are still said by other Greeks to be vindictive, distrustful of strangers and thoroughly unsociable, though they admit their loyalty to their guests. Originally ruled over by some great family like the Mavromichali, each clan tended to live in high towers, whence they waged unending warfare against the next clan in the next tower. Male children were referred to as 'guns', since fighting was a man's sole function in life. Females were mere workers, except at the time of funerals, when the women took over the arrangements and vied with each other in the wailing or dirges known as 'miroloyia'. These 'miroloyia' are still held, and if ever I go back to the Mani, I intend to stay until someone dies and have a jolly good time.

The Maniots that I met were, in fact, the soul of hospitality to me, though I noticed that they distrusted my Greek crew. The most interesting villages that I saw were Kitta—the many towered—Boulargoi and Alika, all within a few miles of Yerolimeni, which was to be our next port of call.

The coastline southwards from Limeni is of surpassing loveliness—if loveliness can be measured in terms of grandeur and a certain menace. There are several bays, but all exposed to the westward. We anchored a few moments in Dyro Bay, where some caves with stalactites and stalagmites have recently been discovered and where one is rowed around them in a somewhat uncaveworthy boat, and we rounded the headland on which one sees the fragmentary ruins of once-powerful Tigani Castle. This great

Venetian fortress, with its sisters at Koroni, Methoni and Pylos, once held this whole region in commercial thrall to Venice. But perhaps the grandest sight of all was the promontory of Cape Grosso just before entering the tiny harbour of Yerolimeni. Its inaccessible peaks and caves had probably, I reflected, not been visited by man for thousands of years.

Yerolimeni itself has all the attractions that only a decaying community can offer. Even the solitary mooring-buoy in its harbour is insecurely moored and I preferred to put out a couple of anchors and my stern as close to the rather inefficient quay as I could. We had the good luck to run into a man with a car, who gave us a lift to Kitta to see the towers. Early next morning the valleys rang with rifle fire as the Maniots took pot shots, not at each other, but at the myriad of migratory birds.

South, ever south from Yerolimeni past the cave where legend says Hercules dragged Cerberus from the underworld (difficult to distinguish among the barren rocks) till finally Cape Matapan hove into sight—except for Tarifa in southern Spain the most southerly land in Europe. We rounded it and turned a page in our voyage. We were in the Aegean.

On course 122, the forgotten island of Kithira—birthplace of Aphrodite—came into sight some 20 miles away. The sea was calm—why not push on? And at last light we made the island's main port called Kapsali, in its extreme south.

When we arrived at Kapsali, I was struck with a sense of remorse at not having explored the various small ports and bays of the Gulf of Lakonia. Henry Denham's guide-book *The Aegean*, which describes them so well, had not appeared then and most of my yachting friends advised against bothering with them. One consoles oneself with reflections such as these.

But Kithira is a 'must' to every yachting tourist. It is incredible how the island is neglected, not only in guide-books, whose authors have mostly clearly never been there, but also by the Greeks themselves. Although there is a Yacht Station at Kapsali, there is no sign of a tourist bureau of any kind, and the islanders never stop complaining that Athens completely neglects them. The roads, mostly built while the British had sovereignty over the island, are excellent and we made a taxi drive to the Monastery of Myrtidiotissa—one of the finest I have ever seen—and to a charming village on a river called Mesopotamos. I also made a quick excursion to Avgo Island (Egg Island) which is an unscaleable 200-ft crag off Kapsali,

Missolonghi

Zakynthos

Patras

Gulf of Corinth

Ionian Sea

Katakolon

Olympia

Piraeus

Nauplion

Salamis

Poros

Navarino
Bay

Pylos

Messini

Kalamata

Aegina

Methoni

Sparta

Kardhamili

Hydra

Githion

Spetsai

Kyparesi

Limeni

Aegean Sea

Yerolimeni

Gulf
of
Lakonia

Port Ieraka

C. Matapan

Monemvasia

C. Malea

Kapsali

Kithira

8. *The Peloponnese*

8. The Bosphorus at Istanbul (By courtesy of the Turkish Tourist Information Office).

9. The approach to the new (southern) harbour at Mytilene seen from the Kastro Fort and looking south.

11. Monemvasia. The old Byzantine village clusters at the foot of Greece's 'Gibraltar'.

10. The Ta Xbiex Marina in Malta, with yachts of many nationalities laid up at the end of the 1965 season.

12. *September Tide* at the quay at Ayvalik.

13. Folegandros. Returning from the village to the harbour.

14. Patmos, The east coast seen from the monastery.

where there is a seal cave and cliffs white with a thousand sea-birds.

The port of Kapsali could be better protected and another British yacht there—the *Freedom*—told me she was a bit worried by the possibility of a southerly, which made the place untenable. In such a case, said her skipper, it would be wiser to sail around to St Nicholas at the island's north-east corner, where, although there was less to see, there was a well-protected natural harbour. I only wished that we had longer to stay in this charming place and that the small excellently sheltered natural inlet next to Kapsali could be dredged deeper than the 2 or 3 ft of water it now offered. Maybe this will happen one day.

Perfect weather favoured us for the long haul eastabout Kithira and inside Dragonera Island (the channel where a ship was wrecked bringing treasures from Greece to the British Museum), and even onwards north to Cape Malea, terror of the ancients. It was here that a great wind arose, driving Ulysses off his course and down to Crete, but we had it flat calm. So calm that we could hear the hermit who lives on the end of the cape ringing his chapel bell in welcome. He is said to live only on the gifts of sailors and I still haven't squared my conscience that we didn't stop and give him at least a loaf of bread.

After a stop in a cove called Port Phutania for lunch and a swim, we found ourselves off Monemvasia—Greece's 'Rock of Gibraltar'—at tea-time. The weather was getting warm and it is a golden rule in these waters never to attempt any sightseeing in the midday period. Not only is everything likely to be closed, but it is too hot for any pleasure. Monemvasia—literally translated is 'one entrance only'—is a strange steep rock with a Byzantine town, mostly in ruins, crowning its top and nestling into its southern side. There is a narrow causeway which connects the whole with the mainland of the Peloponnese. One can shelter on either side of this causeway, depending on the wind's direction. There is a Yacht Station off the southern side, with a mooring-buoy, but I do not advise a protracted stay here.

The ancient town is well worth visiting, although if you want to get to the top a stiff climb is involved. This is best tackled towards sunset, when the light and view are superb. The modern town, on the landward side of the causeway, is without interest, except that it has a post office and a place where ice can sometimes be bought. The mountain, which gives its name to 'Malmsey' wine, is one of the strangest places in Greece, its gaunt brick ruins covering acres of sad seldom-visited territory stretching seaward, bemoaning its great Byzantine, Venetian and Turkish past.

At sunset we left it. Port Ieraka lay just around the corner and extended a welcoming shelter in all weather. The entrance to the inlet is very difficult to spot by day and even the *Admiralty Pilot* gives it a special sketch so you don't miss it. By night there is a green flashing light marking its starboard-hand entrance. If approaching by day, the best plan is to take one's bearings from a conspicuous white chapel a mile north of Point Vathi—one then simply follows the danger-free coast until the opening is in sight. The approach then is on 220. The sound leading up to the village is deep and does not shallow substantially until close to the houses, when an anchor should be dropped and a line put out ashore, for there is very little swinging-room should it come on to blow. There is a lagoon at the head of the sound—all gloriously picturesque—and one can have a splendid picnic on its shores by dinghy. But do not try to use the outboard, as there is too much weed. There are almost no facilities for buying anything in the village—except, of course, the inevitable glass of 'ouzo'—but in fine weather the fishermen often have crayfish for sale. The correct price to pay is Dr.45–50 per kilo. In 'smart' places one often gets asked double this. Port Ieraka, the best shelter on the south-eastern shores of the Peloponnese, is a place that likes to be visited and indeed must be.

Next day northwards. Along a superb coastline to a small village called Port Kyparisi—badly protected, and I was rash to spend the night there, but things turned out safe after all. The crossing towards Spetsai was made after some discussion as to whether we should put into Nauplion or not. I had often been there before, and it is one of the best-protected ports in this part of the world, although the yacht station and the town drain outlet are unfortunately synonymous. It is, moreover, an excellent tourist centre for visits to the ruins of Mycenae, Tyrinth and Epidaurus, apart from what it offers itself in the way of one of the best-situated Venetian 'Kastros' in Greece.

Another school of thought was for making a magnificent natural harbour called Port Kheli, where we had once spent a quiet and moonlit night, but in the end we found ourselves passing through the narrow channel between Spetsai Island and its child, Spetsapoula. The tiny partly wooded island of

Spetsapoula is the property of the Greek shipowner, Mr Stavros Niarchos, and his various yachts—including *Creole*—are often to be seen around these waters. He has had built an excellent artificial harbour, but I do not think one is allowed to land there, except, presumably, on the foreshore.

We called for an hour at Spetsai to look up Sam Barclay, the British yachtsman who has a house there, and is the owner of *Stormie Seas*, a sailing yacht which he had built near Piraeus to his own design. A lot of yachts like to winter here and there is a good slipway. Coming eastwards from Spetsai to Hydra, we had our first blow, a southerly, catching us on the beam and making things uncomfortable. Considering it had been flat calm all the way from Corfu, we could hardly complain. I had, in fact, been prepared to do as I had done on other trips around the Peloponnese, to start each day at 6 o'clock and make one's objective by noon, thus avoiding the wind which invariably blew the whole afternoon. Its direction varied greatly, but it was generally southerly along the eastern coast and northerly on the western. We had been lucky.

Hydra is not everyone's cup of tea. Fast ferries from Athens pour out hundreds of trippers, the quay is lined with rather bogus imitations of St Tropez, mostly filled by foreigners and the '*jeunesse dorée*' of Athens living it up. Genuine locals seem in a minority. 'Colours' and 'sunset' were faithfully rendered by the cadets at a merchant-navy training school and I am glad to say all the yachts took their time properly. Generally, British yachts (at least the genuine ones) in Greek waters pay excellent attention to their flags. One wishes one could say the same for others.

And so through Poros, with its excitingly narrow channel and its Venice-like atmosphere, via Aegina and its gloriously preserved little Temple of Aphaea, to make fast at the new yacht marina at Passalimani in the port of Piraeus. It had been a marvellous trip and fully justified our confidence in the Peloponnese as a cruising area. One gets sick of hearing of people sailing to the Cyclades and having a disappointing trip, 'each island much like the last and an awful wind to make things worse'. The weather around the Peloponnese is seldom anything but fair, the land mass contains almost all the worthwhile sights—Olympia, Bassae, Monemvasia, the Mani, Pylos, Mycenae, Tyrinth and Epidaurus—and if you go the whole way around by using the Corinth Canal, you can throw in Delphi and Nafpaktos. What better way of spending a fortnight?

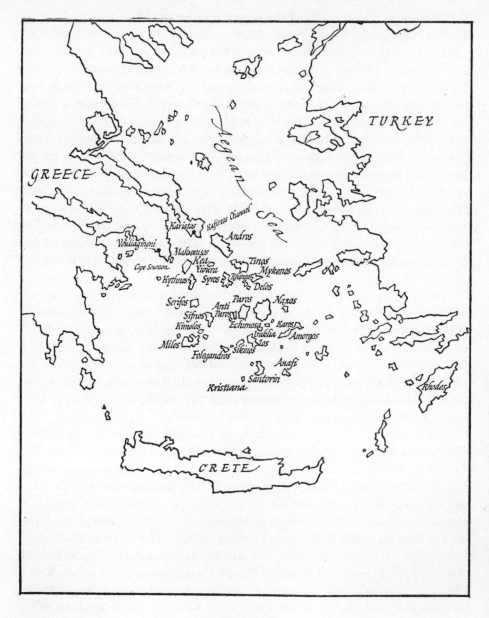

9. *The Cyclades*

But it is essential—and sometimes wise—to visit the Cyclades once. That is the name of the circular group of islands ('kyklos' is the Greek word for a circle—hence the name) in the middle of the Aegean Sea, converging around the sacred island of Delos. Today, the islands are much publicized by Mykonos, which has been developed as a sort of rather eccentric tourists paradise, and by Delos itself, whose ruins, of course, everyone wants to visit. One might add Santorin, another tourist goal; and rightly so, since it is the only active volcano in this part of the world. But here the average tourist's knowledge ends. To him, Paros, Serifos, Sifnos, Naxos and all the rest of them are but names.

Not so to the yachtsman, who can make his leisurely way from island to island, concentrating perhaps, as a yachtsman will do, on the things that not everyone knows. And so it was with delight that we sailed again. And this time it was early in June, when the days are long, the sun is clement and the dread Melteme north wind has not yet started on its midsummer madness.

Before sailing from Vouliagmeni, the splendid new Yacht Marina that the Greeks have so wisely built themselves some 10 miles south-east of Athens, we were lucky enough to have a Malta 'met.' forecast from Basil Mavroleon's *Radiant II* at anchor outside. This was a godsend, for in this part of the world a forecast used to be as rare as an ice cream in Hell, though Athens Radio is now sparing a couple of minutes a day to a plain-language forecast in English. So off we went for the traditional lunch and a swim in the anchorage at Sounion, beneath the ruins of the Temple of Poseidon.

This is often something of a luxury, for the wind, even though not actually a Melteme, can sometimes rise while one is taking one's ease, but should have been pressing on. But we were in luck, and the passage after lunch across the strait to the southern tip of Kea at Cape Tamelos, despite the moderate beam sea from north, was easily accomplished. There is always a bit of a sea off this cape, where waters meet, but with the wind now astern on a new course south to the anchorage in Apokrousis Bay on the north-west coast of Kythnos, the rolling was replaced by a slight yaw as the stern seas followed and broke on us. Loutra Harbour, on the extreme north of Kythnos, is a better harbour once you make it, but in the circumstances Apokrousis seemed preferable. On passage, I had a radio-telephone chat with *Christina* (Aristotle Onassis) to confirm the latest Malta weather. It is a boon to have these big yachts around and hear weather reports from them which are unobtainable on a small yacht's system. And they are always very ready with their help.

Kythnos provides a number of good ports of refuge, but little else. Otto, Greece's first king, tried to make a 'spa' of the local hot springs, but people haven't much use for that sort of thing these days. So course was set for Serifos and the excellent shelter of Livadhi Bay at its bottom right-hand corner. Here there is good holding-ground on sand and the bay is used by quite a number of yachts, mostly because of the shelter, but also because the place is pretty. Wonder of wonders, there is a real sandy beach and a taxi drive up to the 'Khora' or main village of the island overlooking the bay like a Provençal 'village perché' is highly rewarding. Inexplicably, there is no 'Yacht Station', so that one has to fetch one's fresh water by bucket from a village tap and the quay is so encumbered with local craft that it is often difficult to find a berth. But lying off is preferable and safe.

On leaving Serifos, one has the choice of either crossing direct via Anti-Paros to the smaller islands surrounding Naxos—or continuing southwards via Sifnos—home of old-time gold-mines—to distant Santorin and so north again. Two years ago we had done the long circular tour to Santorin, via Sifnos, Folegandros, Ios and so north. Sifnos appeared attractive, but suffered from a lack of suitable anchorages, the seldom-visited Folegandros, though even worse supplied with shelter, did produce a memorable mule-back ride up to its village, which in turn yielded some superb cliff scenery; while Ios, though I cannot speak very highly of its main harbour, offered a number of bays sheltered from northerlies, friendly natives, an un-paralled number of windmills and a somewhat dubious 'Homer's Tomb'. Santorin was certainly the prize exhibit of the round tour. Consisting of an enclosed lagoon-like sea formed by water rushing in through breaches in an extinct volcanic crater, its sheer sides tower menacingly skywards, precariously supporting rows of white villages. In the centre of the 'lagoon' lie the Kaimeni Islands, still smoking sulphurously. An arrival at sunset, when the cliffs are purple in the golden light, is something one does not easily forget. The only snag is that, the crater being so deep, there is virtually no anchorage. By putting one's bowline to a buoy and a stern line to the village quay, one can just spend the night if all goes well, but if it should start to blow, one has to get out—just where to is quite a problem. Most yachts therefore try to base themselves on Ios when visiting Santorin and make a day trip of it.

Spurning the attractions of Santorin, we decided to try something new. And so we found ourselves steering for the southern tip of Anti-Paros, having rounded which and being in calm waters, we anchored for lunch in an inlet on the eastern side of the island called Marmora Bay, after the marble quarries adjacent. From here, it was an easy run down to Echimosa for the night. We had chosen this off-the-beaten-track island to the south of Naxos because we had heard that for long it had been one of the most backward islands of the Aegean. Not until it was visited and 'adopted' by the rich French industrialist Elie Manouri did it get electricity, a harbour and a water supply. We called on the village priest, whose son, a radio-telegraphist in the Greek merchant marine, happened to be at home and translated for us. Later, we had half the village aboard for a farewell nip. Greeks drink very little, so it was not an expensive performance.

It was calm next morning and I decided to attempt the passage of the formidable Agrilos Channel, which would cut off quite a corner on our way to Amorgos, our next objective. As we closed the narrow gap, however, the run of tide through it seemed so frightening that I put about before it was too late, circumnavigated the offending islands of Ophidusa and Dhrima, and got on to my passage course for Katapoula Bay, the only protected harbour in Amorgos.

Amorgos, where the harbour itself is not all that good, turned out to be unpractical from the point of view of living. Wretchedly poor, it offered no fresh water, ice or supplies. But what of it? It boasted a taxi, which took us up to see the magnificent view from the top of the island, whence we hired mules to take us down the other side to see the eleventh-century monastery hewn out of the cliffside. I will never forget this experience. The monastery is the most unique I have ever seen—and I have visited dozens.

So north again, leaving Karos to port on a perfect June morning, the fishing boats motionless on a glassy sea. In the Koupho Channel we stopped and bought our lunch from a fisherman—two fine bream. Except for crayfish, always very reasonable except in the main tourist centres, fish in Greece is not cheap. We anchored in Rhena Bay, on the south coast of

Naxos, and cooked the bream and ate them and swam and lay in the sun and wished we could stay there for ever. Another 3 hours' coasting saw us in Naxos town. The southerly approach must be handled with care, for there are rocks, submerged and awash, in the fairway. One always thinks of Ariadne in this island, but there is little trace of the lady's alleged visit. Most prominent were the ruins of a temple of Apollo overlooking the port.

Most yachts visiting Paros—our next objective—use the main harbour of the island called Paroika. It is well placed for the few island sights, but offers poor protection and the swell seems to enter at the least provocation. Naussa Bay, in the north of the island, is far better, and there we went. This magnificent inland sea offers protection from all quarters once one is inside its two sheltering headlands, good fishing and dinghy sailing and a warm welcome at the little village of Naussa at its head. The actual harbour of Naussa is very tricky of entry and I suppose we were about the biggest yacht ever to use it. Avoid the submerged mole to port on arrival.

I have always sworn that I would not ever go again to Delos and Mykonos—so often have we been there. But they are so much at the centre of things that it is almost impossible when navigating the Cyclades to avoid them. Delos is, in any case, always well worth while in a yacht, for, except during the forenoon, when the Mykonos 'caiques' disgorge their tourists for a morning visit, one has the place to oneself. The antique 'commercial harbour', though it only has 2 or 3 fathoms of water to offer, affords better protection from the Melteme than any other locally. If the moon is full, do everything in your power to spend the night at Delos: you will never forget it.

Mykonos was exactly as I expected to find it; full of foreign tourists of the 'beatnik' variety, the locals harassed and unwilling to do much to help, mailboats arriving every few minutes. The tourist influx has at least had one good effect—it is now possible to get an eatable meal at several local 'tavernas', a change from the rest of the Cyclades. Luckily, the north wind was not blowing, for then the harbour becomes untenable. In such a case, one should go to Ornos Bay—on the Mykonos south coast—where a Yacht Supply Station has been specially erected.

Across to Tinos in a flat calm was a nice change after the horrors of the Melteme weather we had experienced last time we did this trip one August night. Tinos is the Lourdes of Greece and especially on August 15, Feast of the Assumption, it is a focal point for pilgrimages to the magnificent monastery on the hill overlooking the town. Unfortunately, the place has suffered severely from the commercialization that always seems to attend a place of alleged miracles, and the manners of the local population have declined accordingly. But the harbour is excellent and I was glad to note that since our last visit there had been installed a 'Yacht Station'.

Next morning, sailing up the west coast of Tinos, the usual phenomenon of the winds presented itself. As each decline in the land contour was passed, more or less severe gusts blew down on us; at the Dhisvaton Strait, separating Tinos from Andros, however, things were more or less calm and the violent winds again only made themselves felt when we anchored for lunch in a bay on the Tinos north shore. In fact, one must admit that in the Aegean, the lee of an island—at any rate of a high island—is always its windiest side. This phenomenon continued all that afternoon as we crept up the 'lee' shore of Andros; it was only by hugging the coast within a cable or two that we managed to avoid the worst of it.

We eventually made the little resort port of Batsi, where I had intended to spend the night, but the wind by then had gone nor'-west and there seemed too much swell in the harbour to stay there comfortably. We accordingly pushed on a few miles to the Bay of Gavrion, where there is good protection from all winds, and anchored. I noticed with approval that a new quay was under construction there. Why is it that Greece, a poor country with a young tourist industry, is able endlessly to improve her facilities for boats, whereas in France, a country with a great tourist tradition and especially so for yachting on her south coast, does little to improve the yachtsman's lot? The reply might be embarrassing.

Time was marching on. Most of the major Cyclades had been visited. As so often happens in these waters, it was a question of finding the calmest and most interesting way back to the shelter of Cape Sounion. Things looked pretty good and I was tempted to sail direct for Sounion, only a few hours by direct route from where we were. But I was glad we did not, for a most interesting day ensued.

The glass continued to fall and the sky was overcast, though there was not a breath of wind. We determined to try our luck at crossing the notorious Kafireos or Doro Channel, the funnel between Andros and Euboea through which the main shipping arteries between Piraeus and Istanbul pass. We accordingly set course for a small bay on the Euboean coast called Kastri, which was recommended by the Admiralty Pilot. The passage across was uneventful, except for the presence of several large tankers apparently motionless in the ominous calm. While riding at anchor in Kastri, however, a violent swell from south-east developed and we determined to sail for the shelter of Karystos, a small fishing-port south-west about Euboea. Once at sea, we were amazed to find ourselves flung around by waves from all directions, like coming through the Alderney Race. Of wind there was none and I was at a loss to account for the sudden venom of the Aegean. We had to batten down everything, only just in time to avoid being swamped by the seas that broke over us. We managed at length to negotiate the strait inside Mandhuli Island (it bears the big light that marks the entry to Kafireos Channel) and here we observed a north-going current of some 4 or 5 knots. I have never made out whether these confused conditions were purely tidal or whether they had something to do with a distant disturbance, or whether it was a combination of both. At any rate, things flattened out as we approached Karystos, their only aftermath being a long and regular scend in the harbour which sometimes exposed parts of the sea-bed.

Karystos provided excellent shelter, though the town is without the slightest attraction and there is no Yacht Station. During the night, the wind went around from SE. to NW., so that, whereas the first part of that day's trip was accomplished in the lee of Euboea, the second part as we crossed the Gulf of Petalion to the diminutive port of Rafina on the mainland of Attica was a rough affair. I had never been to Rafina before and I pray I may never have to go there again. The pierhead is very difficult to make out, since it consists of the prow of a coaster which has been cleverly adapted for the purpose. There is almost no swinging-room in the tiny port and, since the sea was beating directly into the entry, we had the narrowest of margins as we entered and swung to a berth alongside. I thought for a moment we might even touch bottom and be shipwrecked on the beach. A man with a tanker filled us up with water and tried to charge £1 for it. The ensuing scenes were greatly appreciated by the crowd.

Rafina southwards next morning, however, was a delightful run, as it nearly always is in summer-time, when the winds are virtually sure to be northerly. As we passed Port Raphtis, with the giant figure of the tailor on his stool on an island to welcome us in, I realized we had made a mistake in going to Rafina. I have since heard only good reports of Port Raphtis and will certainly patronize it next time.

The wind dropped away, as we came inside Makronisos Island and Poseidon's Temple on Sounion once more came into view. This is always an encouraging thing to see. I was sorry we had abandoned our plan of visiting Kea, whose port of St Nicholas is vast and well-sheltered despite its inadequate quayage. In the old days, it was a coaling-station for vessels bound north to the Dardanelles. Now it rots quietly, the occasional yacht almost its only consolation.

We were soon around Sounion. The circle of the Cyclades, the Sacred Islands that lie in a circle, had been made.

4

North to the Land of Tito

(with a visit to Venice thrown in)

Corfu in midsummer is a nice place. The forenoons are hot and quiet, but at midday a nor'-west wind rises, reaches Force 4 to 5 by mid-afternoon and is gone by dinner-time. Much the same happens over the road in Brindisi, some 130 miles away, except that the wind is usually there in the morning and gone by the afternoon. In fact, nor'-west, with variations in timing, is the normal Adriatic summer pattern.

I was getting ready for a cruise along the Yugoslav coast and ending in Venice, thankful that the Aegean with its biting summer winds was astern of me and looking forward to the peace and quiet of an Adriatic August. Only the early route remained to be decided. Between Corfu, most northerly Greek port, and Bar, the most southerly Yugoslav port of entry, lay the awkward small country of Albania, with some 150 miles of antagonistic coastline and a claim to a 10-mile territorial sea limit. For a small boat that cruises at 7½ knots, that knows she cannot enter any Albanian port except as a prize, and moreover has little confidence in what the Albanian interpretation of 10 miles might be, the decision to take a detour via Brindisi seemed wise and indeed inevitable. True, I had written at length to 'The Albanian National Tourist Organization' at Tirana (no reply) and received a baby-passing letter from the Albanian Legation in Paris to my requests for a visa, but from what I could gather from my inquiries I was convinced that unless one was Chinese (not from Formosa) one's reception in Albania might be a little old-fashioned. And so instead of 150 sea-miles one's trip via Corfu–Brindisi–Kotor was going to be 258. What matter? So we sailed at 1900 from Corfu one July evening in 1963. My decision to go via Brindisi seemed more than justified when, soon after last light, when we were just clear of the narrow Corfu North Channel, gunfire started on the Albanian coast and we narrowly missed being caught in the glare of Communist (Chinese variety) searchlights. I had just been speaking to Corfu Radio about the weather and wondered whether we had unwittingly provoked these excitements. The big light on Fano Island was

10. *North to the land of Tito*

abeam by midnight (the echo-sounder as one crosses the ridge here is an excellent help to fixing one's position) and we went on to our passage course of 303 for Cape San Cataldo south of Brindisi, whence we were to follow the Italian east coast. The wind held north-west all night, decreasing towards dawn, but always enough northerly in it to justify our steadying sails. San Cataldo, a very low-lying part of Italy, came up as expected and we were in Brindisi for lunch, when we put our clocks back an hour to conform with local time.

The shorter time one spends in Brindisi—a severely practical city—the better. So, after a taxi drive to Lecce—probably the least-known of Italy's 'villes d'art'—watering and a bit of last-minute shopping, we sailed at dusk on course 008 for Kotor Fjord. With the summer north-westerlies persistent as ever, we had a beam sea most of the way: the only shipping sighted was in the traffic lane off the Italian coast.

The high land behind the Yugoslav coast showed up several hours in advance of our being able to make out the coastal marks, so we had ample time to speculate as to our landfall, which, had we continued on our chosen course, would have put us several miles north of the fjord mouth. This may be partly due to the north-going currents along the east coast of the Adriatic. A useful distant mark for making this approach—which is that most yachts from 'foreign' would use, is the saddle peak just north of Lovcen Mountain. To aim south of this saddle should put one reasonably close to Kotor Fjord and the fortress on Cape Ostri (Ostri Rt) later becomes clearly visible, marking the port-hand entry.

Once in the fjord we made for the pleasant little resort of Hercegnovi and asked for clearance. We were told, however, that things had been reorganized since our last visit in 1960 and were directed to a drab small-scale commercial quay a couple of miles up the fjord called Zelenika. This was now the only port of entry and departure in the Kotor area. Clearance was speedy once the right officials had been found and no difficulties were made. I asked if we had to declare our money and was told this was now unnecessary. The rate of exchange had been altered in our favour since I was last here and was now Din. 2,100 to the £, against only 1,120 in 1960, and we all thought this a very fair figure. It is now (1966) Din. 3,500 to the £. That evening, after a glorious run up the fjord, the evening lights turning the great face of Lovcen violet, we made fast at Kotor for the night. As usual, the absurd

Yugoslav regulation governing the issue of an 'Itinerary' to a foreign yacht (called a 'Manifest' in Greece and a 'Costituto' in Italian) had been put into force. We were asked to name the ports we wished to visit. As one had little idea where to go in advance, the only hope was to put down all the places one had ever heard of and hope for the best. They need not be in consecutive order. If you put down a place that was prohibited you would be told so. But no one told you in advance what was not allowed. It was a sort of guessing game, with penalties for the yachtsman but none for the Yugoslavs. If you stopped at a place—which included anchoring in a bay—not on your list you did so at your peril, for it might be a prohibited area. If you wanted a place added some of the larger port harbour masters were authorized to do so, but it was a job to persuade them to do it. The antiquated system, designed, I imagine, to protect a security requirement which under modern conditions it seems impossible to justify, caused so much trouble that I understood the harbour masters were going to try to get it altered. In 1965 a new system of permits for visiting yachts, in the Greek model, was introduced.

Kotor is a 'must' for the intelligent yachtsman and so are the picturesque two islands off Perast adjacent, though anchorage here is difficult owing to the great depths. I recommend dropping anchor between them in about 3 fathoms and putting a stern line to one of them.

Despite the boiling heat there was no ice to be had at Kotor, but the harbour master told us to go to a place called Meljina in the fjord, where there was a factory. While I was ashore, trying to buy the ice, a policeman appeared and told us we were in a military area, although we were assured it was not by the harbour master, and we had to slip feeling rather unwanted.

The coastal run up to Gruz—the commercial harbour of Dubrovnik—was delightful and could be made close inshore. It is galling for a yacht not to be able to use the old harbour at Dubrovnik, but to have to lie in the commercial harbour some 15*s*. worth of taxi from the sights. I wonder whether this injustice will ever be put right. Worse was to have to pay Din. 150 per metre length in harbour dues. Dubrovnik is the only Yugoslav port that charges a yacht to lie there. Fortunately, these irritations were more than atoned for by the beauty of the city itself—once named Ragusa and the origin of the term 'argosy'. We stocked up with duty-free stores

11. *The Yugoslav coast*

here from the excellently run Government ship chandlery 'Brodokomerc'. There was some trouble getting a new 'Itinerary' and Customs papers from the offices, which all closed at 1300, and the confusion over our fishing permits had to be experienced to be believed. In the end we found ourselves paying nearly £1 a day per person for the right to go spear fishing (without air bottles) in the Dubrovnik harbour area alone. Considering that nobody ever sees many fish in these waters (except at very great depths) we all thought this an expensive swindle. The permit has in theory to be renewed at every place one visits at the same rate, so a cruising yachtsman might just as well abandon the idea altogether.

After a quick dash back to Molunat (a permit was issued this time, although at first it was refused) and a glimpse of the Bay of Budva (one of the loveliest parts of the Montenegrin coast), we made a long hop to the island of Mljet, claimed by some to be St Paul's Malta, or Melita. We were just relaxing in the sun at anchor in a charming bay when a naval launch came alongside and told us to be off—another geographical blunder. But it was an 'ill wind', for instead we made for the magnificent fresh-water lake called Veliko Jezero, on the seaward side of Mljet, and found that a canal had been cut joining the sea to the lake, through which we steamed when the tide was right, for the flow of water must be adverse to enable a ship to pass the narrow channel. The lake was superb; we met a Yugoslav yacht which was a great help as a pilot and immensely enjoyed our stay at anchor off the picturesque Benedictine island monastery, which has been converted into an hotel in excellent taste.

Another night in Mljet, Korcula (of which more anon), and we found ourselves in the fascinating group of islands known as Lastovo (or Lagosta in Italian). After a night at anchor in the well-sheltered Porto Rosso bay I was about to weigh when a figure ashore asked to be rowed aboard. I photographed this little party as my hand rowed him toward us and it turned out he was some sort of policeman. After approving our papers he had the nerve to demand my film, since, he explained, photographing policemen in Yugoslavia was not allowed. I thought we would come to blows, so incensed were my shipmates, but in the end I ripped the film out of my camera and gave it him. Some of my better shots were thus ruined, but doubtless bureaucracy was satisfied as its minion made off with a piece of useless celluloid in his pocket.

That evening we went on to one of the prettiest places I have ever yachted to, in another part of the Lastovo group, dropped the hook in a bay and put a stern line to a tree ashore for the night. As dusk fell a severe thunderstorm broke and for hours we were covered in torrential rain. At midnight there was some shouting ashore and I observed two seamen letting go our stern line. We managed to stop them and I ferried them aboard for coffee and sandwiches, during which they explained that we were in a prohibited anchorage and must sail 'forthwith'. Naturally I had to refuse and, after ferrying them some miles away to their barracks, they agreed to compromise if I sailed at first light. There was nothing in our permit to indicate that this particular bay was unauthorized as an anchorage and we were gradually getting less pleased with our trip, where, despite the beauties of the land and sea, 'only man was vile'.

A call at Vela Luka on Korcula Island—a nice unassuming place where fishermen go about their business as though everything were normal—a night at anchor in the enchanted waters of Scedro Island, and we were at Split, a lovely and interesting town, but where the accommodation for a yacht was quite wretched. There was still the excellent Yacht Club, but, presumably as it was also used by the Navy, foreign yachts were barred from it. The least said about the harbour the better, except to note that the harbour master's staff were the soul of kindness and assistance. I paid £10 for some laundry, which we thought a lot.

At the island of Solta some of us went swimming from the dinghy and were fired on by a soldier ashore. This exciting event drove us to protest via the British Consul at Split at not having been warned of a military post. The local inhabitants told us they had also been fired at and the post was quite new. The official reply came back later, somewhat 'à la Russe', to the effect that we could not have been fired on, as there were no soldiers on the island; 'it must have been some fisherman protecting his favourite stretch'. I can only say that it did happen, that we saw the soldiers and that yachts visiting this coast can never be careful enough. Needless to say, our permit for Solta was most explicit.

Navigationally, the most interesting passage on the journey farther north is the approach to Sibenik via the narrow tortuous passage from seaward. As this is a one-way street, fly flag 'Z' and the signal station at either end will signal whether passage is free or not. Sibenik is another touristic 'must' and the passage up the lovely River Krka to the Krka waterfalls above the village of Skradin is another thing one must remember to put on one's 'itinerary'. The Admiralty Pilot, which, by the way, is essential for all these waters, is not very explicit on the upper reaches. My own advice is to anchor off Skradin village and go on up to the falls by dinghy.

From inside Yugoslavia to outside it—or from Skradin to the almost desert island of Kornat, the very edge of the republic—was an interesting bit of navigation among the myriad barren rocks that form this part of the Gulf of Kvarner. We found a tiny fishing hamlet at a place called Lavsa: it was so much what we wanted that we stayed there for three days before sailing—through the narrow Katina and Zrelac straits—for Zadar. I was glad my draught was only 5 ft: otherwise a very much longer detour would have been necessary. At Zadar we came across the new-style glass-fibre motor yacht *Odyssey*, with her owner, Lord Merthyr, skippering, and that evening Mr Kruschev, with his host President Tito, steamed north past the town in an impressive convoy of five or six ships, one of the two escorting destroyers being, I was glad to note, ex-British. Another note of warning; in Yugoslavia one must never, never, never photograph anything resembling a warship or even a sailor (believe it or not). The British yacht *Glorangay* (Gordon Clarke) got into hot water for snapping one of the submarines in this particular convoy.

The islands of Silba and Premuda, which we decided to visit instead of taking in the more conventional stopover places in the Gulf of Kvarner, were found to be unexpectedly beautiful, fitting preludes to the rather dismal port of Pula, which was to be our last Yugoslav port. I had hoped to sail for Venice from Rovinj, a much prettier place further north on the Istrian coastline, but unfortunately this was not a port of departure.

We were leaving Yugoslavia with mixed feelings. Certainly there had been an improvement in living standards since we were last there, but, compared with the happy countries of Greece and Italy, the atmosphere was sad, sad. Everywhere it was 'Bonjour tristesse'. The ports are excellent and Providence has given the Yugoslavs a magnificent coast, ideal for yachtsmen. But one was hamstrung by the regulations and never quite sure of whether or not one was breaking them. Again, one of the worst features was the lack of contact with the population. Yugoslavs, with the exception of harbour masters and others having a job to do aboard, were forbidden to board a foreign yacht. One or two came to see us at my request, but preferably after dark and then they were obviously ill at ease. I am told this absurd rule is made to prevent Yugoslavs escaping. This may well be so, for at several places ashore we were asked if we had a berth for a couple of extra bodies. We naturally always had to refuse, as to take stowaways would have got us into serious trouble not only with the Yugoslav authorities, but also with the Greeks or Italians when trying to land them.

Frankly, we found Pula drab and depressing. The seaward approach was indeed superb and as one entered the magnificent natural harbour, with the fishing-fleet putting to sea and signs of great activity in the shipyards, one did get a sense of exhilaration. This was soon dispelled when one landed. There were some fine streets and buildings, but no life in any of them. There was one nineteenth-century-type palace hotel called the 'Riviera', morgue-like and decaying, not one decent restaurant and life ended at sunset. It was, however, a good shopping centre, and as usual the harbour master's office was kind and helpful, telling us how to buy ice, fuel and fresh water, so that we should be well stocked for the trip across to Italy. Outward clearance by Customs and Emigration was accomplished without difficulty.

Dawn broke gusty and overcast, so that our sailing was delayed until the wind dropped at midday. Marshal Tito keeps a summer house on the Brioni Islands just off Pula and the sailing directions are explicit that a vessel must keep a mile offshore and not even use the channel between Brioni and the mainland. Once on course for the Porto di Lido approach to Venice we found ourselves for a long time in sight of the Istrian coastline, with Rovini clearly visible.

To our surprise, the passage was flat calm. The wind dropped altogether and our main interest became the avoidance of a vast amount of floating debris. It looked to be the sort of stuff that a river in flood could bring to the sea—floating logs, bits of trees and so on. The deep blue of the Adriatic gave way to the dark greens and browns of shallower waters.

Just about when we expected, the big light of Porto di Ponte Vecchia (with a range of 18 miles) turned up on our starboard bow at dusk. All the way across we observed shipping on a parallel course over to port, presumably in the Rijeka–Venice traffic lane.

There are three principal seaward approaches to the Lagoon of Venice, but of these, that known as the Porto di Lido is far the most frequented and I decided to use it. I had never been to Venice by yacht before and the night approach was going to be an interesting piece of navigation. As we came closer, with Ponte Vecchia light flashing ever brighter, the loom of the city began to show up. What appeared to be an unexplained large factory or group of illuminated houses also appeared on my starboard bow and, puzzled at not being able to identify this on my chart, I altered course to port and proceeded along the coast southward. It was moonlight and there seemed to be lights everywhere, so I was confident of making an accurate approach on the landfall buoy established some three miles off the harbour entrance and then getting on course with the shore-based leading lights in line. I was therefore somewhat alarmed when, after staying on this course a good deal longer than I had bargained, no landfall buoy could be seen, despite the clarity of the night. It was obvious by now that I had overshot the mark. When in such a situation, it is no good going doggedly on. One must admit one's error, and put back.

I therefore put about and set course for what I originally thought must be the position of the pierheads. The village drew closer with its thousand lights and with a sudden shock of gratitude I realized the truth—what I had mistaken for an uncharted factory was in truth a couple of dozen merchant ships riding at anchor in the anchorage, awaiting pilotage on the next tide into the lagoon! This admission—which will doubtless lose me much face as a navigator, I give so that others may not have the same unfortunate experience. At length the landfall buoy turned up, a very feeble light I thought, and we were easily able to make out the green and white flash of the starboard-hand pierhead light. Once inside its protection —the wind and sea were rising—we got on to the leading lights and all was well, though the ebbing tide against a light east wind was making for a bit of movement in the channel.

Let me warn the tyro against choosing a night approach to Venice for his first visit. It looks all right on the chart, but, believe me, this was one of the most difficult arrivals I have ever made. Nor were our troubles over. The signal tower to port at the point where one abandons the leading lights and turns to port up the Porto di Lido channel hailed us repeatedly, but, as we did not understand Italian well and anyway could not hear what he was saying, I regret to say that we made no reply. The subsequent

channel passage up the great waterway leading eventually to the Grand
Canal was not an easy matter. It is well marked with light buoys, but as
these have to be distinguished against the thousand twinkling lights ashore,
one normally does not see them until one is close upon them. Add to this
the difficulties created by an endless stream of shipping and ferries rushing
heedlessly across the fairway, and you have an accurate picture of the
pleasures of Venice by Night.

Yachting chums in Malta had suggested that the best berth for us would
be by the bridge near the Public Gardens ferry stop ('Giardini' it is called).
It was not easy to make out just where this was in the dark, but by dint of
going alongside one of the ferry pontoons and picking up a helpful water-
man as pilot (1,000 lire reward) we were able to make fast in what I afterwards learnt was exactly the right berth. Here we passed a truly horrible
night, flung from side to side like a nighmare Ride of the Valkyries as each
successive vessel's wash flung us against the walls of Venice. I did, however,
notice a fresh-water tap ashore: I hear this is about the only one.

I had some trouble persuading the local Customs and police to come and
check us into Italy next morning, but at length they arrived in a smart red
launch and most kindly gave me an Italian chart of the Venice Lagoon.
Proud possessors of this extra information, we decided to make a day trip
in the lagoon to the standard tourist sights of Murano, Burano and
Torcello.

Without an Italian large-scale chart, the trip in the lagoon would have
been impossible. True, the various channels are well marked with dolphins,
but the choice of channel without a chart is more or less impossible. I
again thanked goodness that we only drew some 5 ft, for sometimes I doubt
if we had more than a foot or so beneath us. Burano is an extremely
picturesque lagoon town on the way to Torcello, capital of this whole
region before Venice ever was built. Nowadays it consists of nothing more
than a superb red-brick cathedral and a few unusual old houses. Murano,
much easier of approach, is the famous glass-blowing centre. From Torcello
to Murano and so back to Venice the channel passes through an exposed
part of the lagoon where there is clearly very little water. Imagine our
horror at seeing a large Italian lagoon ferry bearing down on us and
taking up almost the whole of the dredged channel! Although in Venice
proper, for reasons of paddling, traffic keeps to the left, on the lagoon the

ordinary rule of the road at sea applies. I therefore lay off on the outer edge of the canal and awaited my doom. It came. The ferry hardly slowed down. As she passed us, the suction took away all water from beneath my craft and we heeled dangerously over, fast on the exposed lagoon mud. I noticed her skipper shrieking with laughter—the Italians were always famous for their sense of humour, since the days of those odd Borgia dinner parties.

As we drew near to the City of Saint Mark on our return journey. I became increasingly agitated about where on earth we were to spend the night. I could not face the Grand Canal area again, so after a feverish study of the Italian chart we decided to plump for the Arsenal harbour, which seemed reasonably central and quiet. Again fate intervened. A policeman at the entry warned us that this was military terrain and so out we had to go. Darkness was approaching and I was beginning to feel a good deal less happy until we once more had an inspiration. The Italian and Yugoslav charts of Venice both showed a small harbour quite close at hand behind the Sant' Elena Stadium. The chart showed only a few feet of water, but I thought it worth risking and we made the difficult entry against the incoming tide. Imagine our joy when we sighted the masts of many yachts and a group of suitably sporting-looking people ashore waving us in. All our problems were solved.

The 'Diporto Velico Veneziano'—for so it was called—was one of the best yacht clubs we have visited in all these years of wandering. True, it boasted no magnificent clubhouse or grand façade, but the secretary and staff could not do enough to help us. We were given an excellent berth against the piles, but close enough to get ashore by using our side companionway, there was a fresh-water tap adjacent, the water was clean and —oh praise the Lord—it was quiet. To get to Saint Mark's by public transport took about 20 minutes and consisted of a 5-minute walk along a canal to the Sant' Elena water-bus stop, a very short wait and another 10 minutes to Saint Mark's in the ferry. There were all the shops one wanted right at hand and Mario and Rolando, the club boatmen, saw to it that we got all the service we needed.

I almost forgot to mention that there was an excellent small slipway and boatyard right alongside. I profited from this to have a few minor repairs done and to haul our dinghy ashore for repainting. *Odyssey* (Lord Merthyr) arrived a day or two later and the two boats ultimately lay adjacent. Another interesting British yacht was a small sailing boat filled with young soldiers on an 'Adventure training course'. They were stationed in Germany and had brought their boat down on a trailer to Trieste, whence to parts of Yugoslavia and thence over to Venice. The British Consul asked us to drinks and sent his launch for us—all gloriously maritime.

We were in Venice for some 10 days. I can confidently recommend any yacht of not more than 60 ft in length and not drawing more than 6 ft to use the Yacht Club at Sant' Elena. There is quite a big rise and fall of tide here—some 5 ft, I would say—so it is best to arrive near high water. But unless you are a really big boat, do not attempt to lie at the 'Giardini' ferry station. Worse still, do not go where the Venetians seem keen you should— which is the standard yacht berth off Santa Maria della Salute at the entrance to the Grand Canal. *Shemara* (Sir Bernard Docker) arrived while we were in Venice and lay there with a stern gangway to the shore and seemed comfortable enough. But not everyone is as big as *Shemara*. I did note a few yachts up at this berth being flung from side to side in diesel-oil-covered water, with no contact with the shore except by dinghy—a rough passage. We took the opportunity of this quiet berth to repaint and I had a new refrigerator installed. My 'Pinta' automatic pilot, which had been troublesome for lack of expert servicing, was repaired by a representative of the firm who—a real *deus ex machina*—happened to be passing by.

Passage back to Yugoslavia and Pula was again a quiet affair. Its roughest part was at the Porto di Lido pierheads, where tide runs out against the wind. The 'Adventure training' boys confirmed this. Rovinj and Brioni came up as expected and once more we found ourselves entering the enfolding arms of Pula breakwater.

The Yugoslav officials seemed delighted to see us again and indeed we were also very pleased to have them aboard. Glad cries of 'Giveli' and so on were, however, rudely interrupted when it was disclosed that we had some £60 worth of their dinars in our possession. Although I imagined I explained fairly well that these had all been acquired legally on our trip up the coast a month ago, this seemed insufficient for the local financial wizard, who bagged the lot. This was hardly a good start to the homeward trip and I was at pains to express my displeasure. But once the bureaucratic machine has been activated, it is wellnigh impossible to stop it. Although

I was given various bits of paper in exchange, the money did not arrive at my bank until six months later. Seriously, however, be warned against taking out of Yugoslavia more than the Din. 3,000 you are allowed to take in and out. They administer the regulations very haphazardly, but it seems that innocence is no excuse and certainly no safeguard. Had I been asked on leaving Pula 10 days previously, I would, of course, have declared and deposited the money there for our next visit. Write to your M.P. about it.

Owing to our money troubles, we spent a day longer in Pula than we meant, and so had time to visit the extraordinarily well-preserved Roman amphitheatre capable of seating 23,000 people avid for the destruction of Christians. I would have liked to see the arena full of Yugoslav Customs-men and lions. All the officials were very sympathetic to us in our financial extremity, but it was, of course, not much help. We decided to sail south-wards at first light.

The harbour master at Pula had made out a splendid 'itinerary' for us with which to go south. He had put in far more places than there was any hope of visiting, especially as we had determined not to bother with big ports like Rijeka or obvious 'tourist traps' like Opatija (Abbazia). I had, in fact, made up my mind to take the southward journey along the Yugoslav coast more in the capacity of an 'average tourist' than as an enterprising yachtsman; that is to say, I was going in principle to sail from port to port as indicated in my 'itinerary' and seldom stop at out-of-the-way places not specifically mentioned in it. This indeed produced far less trouble: on the return journey, we were only once asked for our papers in an anchorage, as against five separate 'incidents' on the way north a month previously.

Passing outside Porer Lighthouse after leaving Pula (it is wiser not to attempt the inside channel) we set course for our first objective, the island of Susak, which soon came up through the haze. Susak is noted for its wines (not good by our standards), its cultivation of the bamboo and the curious dress of its womenfolk. We were lucky to be there at the time of the wine harvest. The port was only just big enough to accommodate our 54 ft length and manoeuvring inside it to turn around was quite something. The place merits half a day, so one is glad to have the charming wooded island of Losinj, with its excellent shelter in the Bay of Mali Losinj, at hand for the next night stopover.

As we rounded the headland leading into Mali Losinj Bay, the full impact of the gloriously placed town of Mali Losinj left us gasping with pleasure. The bay is one of the best anchorages in Yugoslavia and the authorities have been trying to develop the island as one of their leading resorts—a policy to some extent followed by the Italians before them. Ciano and Mussolini both had villas there, although it is difficult to make out which they were. Both are hotels now and other hotels are building. The island is nevertheless big enough to take quite a lot of development without being spoilt. Some English friends with a car drove us to the St Tropez-like port of Veli Losinj on the inner side of the island and to Cikat Bay, where most of the hotels and villas are located. If there had been time, I would have sailed the yacht around the island to explore some of the anchorages, and I don't think there would have been any trouble with the authorities, except possibly at the western end of Mali Losinj Bay, from which one yacht had been expelled.

All these outer islands of the Gulf of Kvarner are famous for the seamen they produce. A speciality seemed to be yacht hands, for some of the men to whom we spoke ashore told us they had been in foreign yachts in the Mediterranean and longed to get another job of this kind. In the 'pub' on Susak, for example, we were amazed to see a highly coloured view of Cannes Harbour, apparently a familiar sight to the locals.

By paying Din. 500 (about 5s.), we had the bridge across the narrow channel intersecting Losinj island near Mali Losinj opened for us (it would have been free between 0700 and 1400) and managed to get through without accident despite the vagaries of the current which changes its direction every quarter of an hour. The 3-hour passage over to Rab Island was calm and uneventful, except for the negotiation of the shallows near a rock called Mazunel, which was clearly marked on our Admiralty chart, but which we never observed, even awash, although we looked for it closely.

Rab was full of German tourists, had a nudist beach for them, and was obviously proud of its thirteenth-century cathedral and patrician houses of the Venetian epoch, now mostly turned into hotels and restaurants. We were at last able to give a party aboard, our guests being from the Dutch yacht *Eklow* (Mr and Mrs H. G. Wolke) also alongside, assorted Germans, and one Yugoslav, who managed to get a police permit to come. The Wolkes, who have business interests in Yugoslavia, told me they were leaving their yacht for the winter at a little place called Punat on the island of Krk. I would not have cared to do this myself as things were, but, if ever the Yugoslavs should decide to normalize their yachting regulations and make foreign boats really welcome, I would seriously consider leaving *September Tide* to winter in a place like Split, where the facilities seem to me excellent.

By now we had learnt to distrust the guide-book as to at least half of its information. Why doesn't someone write a really factual guide-book to Yugoslavia? It has been done for Greece. For this reason, we decided against going north to Krk or Cres—or even Senj (traditional home of the dreaded 'Bora')—although they were all in our 'itinerary', and set course south for the inland sea of Novigrad. *Crin Bleu* (John Schlesinger) had been there a year or two before and given me good reports of it.

The coastal run down to Novigrad was lovely. It was still September and I had little fear of a Bora developing, although we were always on the look-out for the little fleecy clouds atop the mountains which are supposed to herald its approach. In winter, this coast is the worst Bora stretch and local craft would only navigate in daylight and then as close inshore as possible.

The approach to the Sea of Novigrad is through a majestic sea-canyon spanned at its southern end by a vast new bridge. The strait is called Meslenica and the bridge carries the new coastal road running from Rijeka down to Dubrovnik and points south.

Novigrad itself lay up a creek at the head of the Sea of Novigrad, an altogether delightful small village crowned by a castle said to have been once a favourite haunt of Elizabeth of Austria. The appearance of the place has been somewhat spoiled by the building of one of those square box-like concrete Government hotels at the creek entrance and by the complete disappearance of all the little bars and restaurants that previously gave life to the quay. The inhabitants explained sadly that, with a turnover tax of 60 per cent, the State had deliberately put them out of business.

Our arrival at Novigrad was something of an event and the harbour master volunteered to pilot us up the Zrmanja River next day and into the Sea of Karin as well. We were delighted with this arrangement and so, I think, was the harbour master, who remained at the wheel throughout, 'à la recherche du temps perdu'. The scenery in the river was starkly impressive in contrast to the undulating cosiness of the land around the

Karin Sea, where we were graciously received by the Franciscan monks at Saint Pasquale's monastery and offered some of the local wine. I had a small motor repair done at Obrovac, the town on the Zrmanja River. On getting back to Novigrad, we were favoured with a visit by the harbour master's family for drinks aboard. They did not stay long, as there seemed to be some doubt as to whether even a harbour master can bring his children aboard a foreign yacht, but it was at least a gesture. Everybody in the little town was charming to us and we left feeling that we had made some friends, even if we should never see them again.

Nin is a decaying medieval town, once the capital of Croatia. I was determined to see it, for its associations with Bishop Gregory of Nin, whose statue by Mestrovic is one of the glories of Split. The approach along the inland channels from Novigrad is very easy, being all clearly marked by lights (not on the Admiralty chart, but all in the Admiralty Pilot). One has to anchor off Nin, as there is not enough water to go close and even dinghying inshore can be tricky, as the boat channel is not marked. The cathedral and the Venetian walls, exactly as they were the day they were blown up at the approach of the Turks, make the place well worth a day trip. To shorten our voyage down to Zadar, I decided to attempt the extremely difficult Prevlaka Channel. As we were weighing, a boatload of soldiers came alongside demanding to see our papers, and I was glad that we had included Nin in our 'itinerary', for they made no trouble.

No sooner were we inside the Prevlaka Channel than we ran aground. I was about to abandon the whole attempt and take the route north about Vir Island, when a sand-boat working near by offered pilotage and her skipper, whom I dropped at the next village, took us safely through.

There ensued a night at Zadar for watering and stores, followed by an early departure for Biograd through the inshore leads. The relative Admiralty chart 1561 was found to be very incomplete, as the majority of the lights and marks in this important channel were not marked. Biograd and the adjacent holiday camps, which the harbour masters all seemed so keen we should visit, were without interest, except for a refreshing swim off one of the camps, and so we pushed on, determined to make Sibenic that night. There was just time to anchor off the highly organized fishing-centre of Murter for lunch. This is the area which acts as a central depot for all the inshore fishermen of the region and is full of curious and picturesque

15. A grouper caught in some 3 fathoms of water off Skiathos.

16. *September Tide* at anchor in a sheltered bay in the south of Naxos.

17. Paxos, one of the
most delightful of the
Ionian Islands, also
possesses a well-
protected natural
harbour (By courtesy
of the Greek National
Tourist Office).

things. We would have stayed longer had the harbour been easy of access and cleaner. As it was, we weighed and sailed through the narrow Tjesmo Bridge passage, the bridge swinging for us for the fee of Din. 500. Thereafter we were in familiar waters until we made fast at Sibenic. We reflected again how pleasant and valuable it was to have a small boat with a shallow draught in these enclosed waters—otherwise, our passage that day would have been much prolonged.

It was blowing hard from the south next morning—the first wind we had experienced for weeks—and I began to wonder whether it might go south-east and turn into a Sirocco lasting several days. At sea, however, it was less strong than in port, and we felt pleased at having decided to try for Trogir after all. Had it continued to blow, we could have put in either at Primosten or Rogoznica, just two of the many coves along this stretch of indented coast.

We made Trogir—the finest 'ville d'art' of all Dalmatia—at dusk, the hour of enchantment when spirits walk. The arrival is a mixture of La Rochelle and Paradise (yachtsman's variety). One can spend a long time in this little town, unspoiled by the hand of successive occupations, a conglomeration of winding cobbled streets, churches and rich carvings. We felt more at home in this lovely atmosphere than at any other port on the coast. I hate buying souvenirs, but I could not resist a plaque of Kairos, God of the Opportune Moment, which most suitable reproduction now presides over my chart-table. The god is a young man running, with head shaved behind, but with a long forelock. You cannot recapture what is past —time must be seized by the forelock. Only at Trogir does it stand still.

The British Consul at Split told me he had only negative news from Belgrade about our proposed return via Albania, a course that everyone seemed to deprecate. We spent an enchanted evening at Milna, a small fishing-port on Brac Island, before calling at Hvar for a few moments next day to take some photographs *en route* to Korcula for the night. At Korcula, where the beautiful old harbour beneath the city walls is so exposed to the prevailing north winds, the Yugoslavs have recently built another quay, facing south and protected by the mass of the city. One now therefore has the choice of either of these two, or of anchoring in the absolute protection of neighbouring Luka Bay. Artistically, this town with its superb Venetian abbey and walled embrasure, is a place not to be missed, overpopulated as it can be by tourists in the season.

Another visit to Dubrovnik, this time tempered by a few hours at the island of Lopud, where we found the only genuine sandy beach we had seen in all Yugoslavia. Fuel and water were again shipped and *September Tide* put out for Cavtat, only a few miles south. Deserted in winter and overfull with visitors in summer, Cavtat's main distinction is that it is not only perfectly lovely, but was formerly where the great shipping families of Banaz and Racic had their houses. Needless to say, these have been transformed into hotels and Government rest-houses, but the atmosphere of civilization still lingers. We made fast at the quay in the main harbour, but the swell, even though it was calm, was so great, that we made use of the harbour master and some of the locals to pilot us that evening around to a sheltered bay adjacent, where we spent a quiet night at anchor.

It was getting near the time when we should have to decide whether to risk detention in Albania for the sake of seeing a new country or go back via Brindisi to Greece, the way we had come. My thoughts on passage southwards to the Kotor Sound were much preoccupied with this. We spent a night of thought at Hercegnovi and next morning, having failed to get any sort of weather forecast, took the bit between our teeth, cleared from next-door Zelenika (my last piece of Yugoslav paper was the departure permit) and set course at 1015 for distant Brindisi. By 2 o'clock next morning we were fast at our old berth in Brindisi opposite the International Hotel. The first question the Italian police asked me was 'Have you any clandestine passengers?'

5

Adventure in Anatolia

'September Tide' heads east in search of fresh fields to conquer
and finds herself
on the edges of a new Turkish wonderland

It was a lovely still summer day when Diana and Trevor joined me aboard *September Tide*. In the Aegean, summer days are not always exactly still, but this was the first day of June and June is an excellent month in these waters. Vouliagmeni, to date the most efficient and pleasant of the Greek yacht stations, was our point of departure. Even Greece was beginning to seem repetitive. So I was glad to find friends who were as keen as I was to explore the regions eastward.

As we slid out of the bay I decided, although it was already a late Attic afternoon, to press on to the anchorage off Cape Sounion for the night. True, it was only 2½ hours away, and it would have been nice to have stayed for drinks and a gossip with one's chums, but, by getting to Sounion that night, we were that much farther on our way—and one never knows. Greek 'met.' reports were at that time non-existent and one's own reading of the weather seemed always to leave something to be desired. Since those far-off days the Greeks have obligingly included 'met.' reports in English twice daily on their radio broadcasts—how one wishes the Italians would copy their example!

And so at dusk to noble Sounion, with the gentle moon bathing Poseidon's temple with her life-infusing light—only to die at dawn as we climbed up the cliff-face to pay homage before slipping for Mykonos. This passage is notorious for its summer difficulties, but that day the sea-god—assuaged perhaps by our prayers at his shrine that morning—was kind to us and all

Skyros

Aegean

EUBOEA
Khalkis

GREECE

Athens

Andros

Piraeus   Vouliagmeni

Aegina   Kea   Yiaora   Tinos

C. Sunion   Kithnos   Syras

St. George   Rhinea   De

Hydra   Serifos   Paros

Spetsai   Sifnos   Antiparas

Milas   Sikinas

Folegandras

Kythera   Santorini

Krist

Antikythera

CRETI

Ayvalik

Mytilene   Pergamum
Dikili

T U R K E Y

Izmir

Ephesus
Samos   Kuş Adası
Tigani
Priene
St. Paul's Bay   Miletus
aria   Gaidaros   Didymus
Fournoi   Arki   Kazakli
Patmos   Lipsas   Jassus
Farmakonisi   Güllük
Leros   Mindas   Bodrum
Kalimnos   L. Koycegiz
Caunus River
Kos   Marmarice   Caunus
Amorgos   C. Krio   Cnide   Fethiye
alaea   Nisiros   Simi   Xanthus
Tilos   Gemili Is.   Kalkan
Alinia   Rhodes Town   Kaş
Khalki   Patara   Kekova
RHODES   Castellorizo
Lindas

Karpathos

Kasos

day long our ship's reflection was mirrored in the perfect stillness of an
Aegean summer sea.

The night in Mykonos—in the wrong berth: I admit on purpose, because
I hate the long walk round to the yacht station. Where I come from we
would have been sent off with a flea in our ear, but here the soft Greek
admonitions not to do it again sufficed—another time, if you please—
'moor in the correct place'.

Delos at dawning—avoiding the forenoon wave of tourists—and by
breakfast we were on our way Patmoswards. In the four seasons that I have
been cruising the Eastern Mediterranean, I had never visited this island,
nor indeed had any of us; and the thrill of discovery pulsed through us all
as we rounded Cape Ilias, its southern extremity, with the superb anchorage
soon afterwards opening up: it was already dark and the fixed red light on
Patmos Town quay was either unlit or invisible. These smaller local lights
are often untended in Greece and should not be relied upon: similarly, I
see that I have logged that the dangerous Skopelos Tragos reefs outside the
anchorage (on this approach one steers between them and the island) were
unmarked and unlit.

Patmos Yacht Station can only accommodate one yacht at a time, but
luckily there was none there and we soon made fast with the aid of Aleko,
the boatman. To our surprise, we were charged 5 drachmae (about 1s. 3d.)
in port dues. Patmos and Monemvasia are the only places in all Greece
where one is still subject to these petty annoyances. The shops ashore
obviously did a thriving trade in souvenirs with the passengers from the
cruise liners that called there and we noticed that Turkish pounds were
offered for sale at something like 25 per cent discount below the official
rate: it was impossible to find out whether this was legal or not.

Patmos is a unique island in that it offers a yacht perfect natural protection combined with plenty to see ashore. The several little townships are
charming, there are excellent bathing bays and the two main 'sights', the
cave where St John wrote *Revelations* and the great fortress-like monastery
crowning the hill—after Athos the most important in Greece—are both
touristic 'musts'. A taxi drive easily covers both in a morning and costs less
than £1. It is, by the way, important to lay out two anchors in this
anchorage, to ensure against the sudden gusts, especially from nor'-west
in summer.

On passage over the 33 miles to Samos the same afternoon, we were delighted to see our old friend *Vileehi*, with Walter Ackermann as usual at the helm, on a reciprocal course. Tigani, the ancient port of Pythagorion, is much the best harbour in Samos for a yacht to use; it also has the advantage of being a port of clearance for vessels coming from the adjacent Turkish coast or going to it. True, the ancient Doric column mentioned by Henry Denham in his book *The Aegean* has been removed, so one can no longer boast to one's friends that one's stern-lines were made fast to a bit of old Greece, but the charming little port is very close to the ruins of Heraion, in a mournful but impressive setting, and to what is probably one of the most important engineering marvels of Hellenistic times, the celebrated underground aqueduct of Eupalinion Orygma. On all fours and in darkness some way inside this Edgar Allan Poe sort of passage, one can pinpoint the place where, 2,000 years ago, workmen, hacking their way towards each other from either side of the mountain barring spring from town, made joyous contact with each other within inches of the level of perfection. Had Pythagoras perhaps something to do with this?

Samos reminds one of the English countryside at its summer best, with perhaps a touch of Burgundy thrown in as one winds along the vineyard-laden roads to its capital of Port Vathy. I took the trouble to buy some Turkish currency at a discount (one is allowed to import up to 200 Turkish pounds—about £10—into Turkey per person) but wondered afterwards whether it had been worth while. Outward clearance from Tigani was easy; just a signature on my abandoned 'Manifest' and we were on our way through the 2-mile-wide Samos Strait which separates the island from the mainland of Turkey. There is a north-going current here and the chart shows some tide-rips, but in practice none of this means anything. A Greek naval patrol vessel was observed which, in view of the tense Turko-Greek relations over Cyprus, was hardly surprising. In the old days they used to say of a Greek they wanted to get rid of 'Send him to Samos'. It was the equivalent of a death sentence, so frequent were the Turkish raids. Nowadays, there seems to be very little contact with Turkey.

It was 22 miles of perfect weather for us to get from Tigani to Kuş Adasi (translated literally as 'Bird Island'), the new port which the Turks have recently completed just north of Samos. At one time there was only an anchorage, viewed with some alarm and discouragement by the

Admiralty's *Mediterranean Pilot*: later on, the Turks built a pier to accommodate the tourist steamers that started to come for a visit to Ephesus, and in the past year or two they have added a short mole at right-angles to the existing pier and near to its root. This forms a small harbour, suitable, I should say, for vessels up to 100 ft in length and not drawing more than 8 ft. The bottom is sand and mud. All this was new since Henry Denham's otherwise excellent sailing directions in *The Aegean* and I made a note to tell him of it. A fixed red light, visible for at most two miles, marks the end of the new mole.

Even more satisfactory than finding a nice new harbour at this spot, which is normally the prey of a ceaseless onshore swell, was the warm and relatively efficient welcome from the Turkish port authorities. They were evidently used to tourists here and a representative of the local agency (speaking fluent English) was soon aboard to take all the worry of the port formalities off our shoulders. A taxi was soon arranged and we managed a memorable drive to Ephesus and the adjacent sites of the Tomb of St John and the 'house of the Virgin Mary' before it was dark. Little remains of the great Temple of Diana (or Artemision) at Ephesus, but the rest of the city offers a vast theatre, a smaller 'Odeon', a marble shopping street, with another street of superb baths. But perhaps the most impressive feature of all was the immensely long street, its marble slabs still negotiable by our little old taxi. Lined with magnificent columns, it once led down to the port of Ephesus. The sea all along this part of the world has retreated, like a courtier bowing before past Imperial glories, so that Ephesus, in the time of St Paul a great seaport, is now stranded inland. I was told that the Turks intend one day to reopen this antique harbour for yachts. What a magnificent thought—like holding the Olympic Games in the Stadium at Olympia—but I fear I shall not be there to sail my *September Tide* up through the mists of time to the routes the Apostles trod.

Kuş Adasi is far preferable for a yacht to visit than Izmir, where we had suffered untold indignities some years back. Not only is it cleaner, but the Turks are glad to see you and put no difficulties in your way. It is an excellent centre for excursions to such places as Priene, Miletus and Didymus, all of which we visited during our stay. These fascinating Hellenic cities, once great maritime centres, now stand at some distance from the sea which once surrounded them. Only the outlines of their

18. Yerolimeni. A Greek shooting party visits our yacht.

19. Psara harbour looking north and showing the old quay.

20. *September Tide* alongside the British compound in Famagusta. The army yachts usually lie here.

21. The disused lighthouse at Beirut now houses its hospitable yacht club.

harbours are still visible, overgrown with fig trees and the wild grasses of the windy plains. Past Priene and Miletus flows the winding River Meander, which gave its name to the river god Meander whose statue is at Miletus, still peering gloomily through the ruins of the ancient baths. A taxi for a day trip to Priene, Miletus and Didymus costs about £10 sterling and is well worth it, though a trifle exhausting along the hot and dusty roads.

Nothing remains of Didymus but the ruins of the great Temple of Apollo, once the seat of the local oracle and a great centre of pilgrimage. Near it are some superb sandy beaches, finer than any we saw in Greece and quite deserted. I had a few years ago meant to sail along this intriguing coast, stopping the night at one of the many bays the chart shows and going thence by taxi or on foot to visit these and other little-known monuments. But, as soon as I got to Kuş Adasi, I realized that this was not practical and it was best to visit all the coastal sites from a convenient port such as Kuş Adasi itself. For not only was one unfortunately still liable to have trouble with the Turkish soldiery—generally illiterate and often suspicious—but, even if allowed to land without questioning, it was wellnigh impossible to summon any kind of transport. 'Get me a taxi' was not a phrase in current use.

At Kuş Adasi fresh water was available at Krs. 50 a ton (about 6*d*.) but it was not recommended for drinking. There was no duty-free fuel, but there was an ice factory on the quay and fresh provisions were on sale at very reasonable prices. Harbour and entry dues were minimal and so was the agency fee (doubtless influenced by the fact that we were also taxi hirers!). I can honestly say that, throughout this Turkish trip, we were never once swindled. Indeed, when we offered more, the money was politely refused—very different from conditions in most of the Mediterranean.

Because of all we had heard of the troubles experienced when cruising this coast and because we wanted to visit several out-of-the-way spots, I thought it best to get the agency in Kuş Adasi to give me a piece of paper to wave at anyone who might be troublesome. This they did. I have no idea what it said, but I gathered that it asked people to be nice to us. I wondered, when we finally slipped at 1100 one sunlit morning (no clearing troubles) whether our good luck would hold.

The run southwards through the narrow Samos Strait was enlivened by the interest shown in us by a Greek patrol craft. I was about to hoist my number as she made for us, but she soon put about and we continued our peaceful journey to St Paul's Bay (did he really land here?) and thence with a following wind and sails set. While we were at anchor for lunch in St Paul's Bay a Turkish patrol boat put in and I was glad to have my piece of Turkish paper with me in case of trouble. These waters are none of them forbidden territory, but, with things as uneasy as they were then between Greece and Turkey, there was always the possibility that any foreigner might be unkindly treated, for the Turks were notable xenophobes.

The prevailing NNW. wind had meanwhile sprung up and sheet lightning lit a darkening sky. The main thing was to get somewhere sheltered for the night. On the chart, the best place seemed to be the Bay of Kazakli, along past the temple at Didymus which we had visited by taxi the previous day, and it was for this that I made. It was an easy bit of navigation, the only hazard being the avoidance of the shoal waters northwards of Tek Agac lighthouse, which stands at the end of their present seaward advance. All along this coast the sea is receding, leaving once-prosperous harbours high and dry. In some cases, as at Heraklea far inland, one even sees bits of the Aegean, complete with coastline and even a small harbour or two, which have got left behind as the sea shrugged its shoulders and gave up the struggle. I do not know the reason for this mournful process: maybe it has something to do with the northward general drift of currents in this part of the Mediterranean meeting the southgoing Dardanelles current out of the Black Sea, a clash occurring and both currents going off westwards.

Kazakli turned out to be nothing very much beyond a sheltered bay with good holding-ground, but this was just what we wanted. Far from being hostile, the natives turned out to be very accommodating. The local authorities came aboard, drank whisky (this is against their religion, but I suppose politeness and the anxiety to 'Westernize' themselves gained the day) and, despite the impossibility of conversation, invited us to shift berth nearer the pier. With two anchors out, I felt secure enough to decline. And so the stormy night passed, giving way to noises off as local fishermen arrived to sell us good Turkish fish. The prices were very low compared with Greece, where fish is considered a delicacy commanding a higher price than meat, and we bought freely. Again, conversation was impossible.

This is the case, with rare exceptions, all along the Anatolian coastline. It is amazing what one can achieve without any 'lingua franca' to fall back on. Cigarettes are, of course, a common currency.

At the back of our minds, we had meant to go direct from Kazakli to Bodrum (formerly Halicarnassus) or to the Greek island of Cos, but the wind next morning showed no inclination to drop; so, half-way across, I decided to alter and make for the historic inlet of Jassus, sometimes now known as Asim Limani. Once an important Hellenistic settlement, this place was later fortified by the Venetians: since then it has fallen into decay, except for its quiet charm, which has probably increased. The harbour entry is only 20 yards wide, and lies between a ruined Venetian tower (to which one should keep very close) and the invisible remains of a sunken mole. These only come into view when one is virtually on top of them, making the passage hazardous at night. Admiralty Chart No. 1606 gives an excellent description, except that it does not show the small pier at the head of the inlet. To this we made fast a stern line and, securely at anchor, went ashore to look at Greek and Venetian remains. This was something of a test occasion, for we had no specific permit for Jassus from our friends in Kuş Adasi, but to our great surprise we were not in any way molested, the locals being completely indifferent to our presence. I gained the impression on this and similar occasions that the Turkish population is, in fact, quite uninterested in yachts and tourists in general. It is only the soldiers who are ever likely to cause trouble. Even port authorities seem to confine their activities to their own precincts. We bought some eggs and vegetables for next to nothing: the local hovels were incredibly poor and dirty, though the Turks themselves had a natural dignity which we admired.

It was clear by now that the general pattern of daily weather in the Aegean must be observed. Winds were inclined to spring up, usually from the north, any time after 1100 and to continue until after sunset. The nights and early mornings were conversely calm. So it was that we sailed from Jassus at first light, as soon as one could make out the remains of the Venetian fort and sunken mole. By breakfast-time we were in Myndos cove, so well described by Henry Denham in *The Aegean*. As our anchor rattled out, I could see some Turkish soldiers ashore with their binoculars trained on us. As we rowed ashore in the dinghy, I expected a volley of questions, but none ensued and the young Turks were soon swimming around us, seemingly accepting us as part of the landscape. We were in no doubt that conditions for yachting in Turkey had greatly improved since we were last there. We bought some absurdly cheap vegetables and a loaf of bread, which we found excellent everywhere. Myndos, which is a good yacht berth, is well described in the relative Admiralty Pilot, but I would say that the entrance is even narrower than described, due to the existence of sunken rocks to port on entering. Leaving Cos to the westwards, we arrived in Bodrum the same afternoon. It had been an interesting run down the Cos Channel, which is an international shipping highway.

I had not been to Bodrum for some years and my memories of it were unhappy, in that the officials there had been especially tiresome, even by Turkish standards. So it was with pleased surprise that we found ourselves being accorded V.I.P. treatment. In return, we made an extravagant shopping sortie to the local souvenir shop, apparently owned by the chief Customs official, Diana going to town in the slipper department and me finding myself wrapped up in Turkish towelling. Through some Americans, the Turks were at pains to impress on us that we were welcome there and that we were not to be frightened by reports of events in Cyprus. I went to some trouble to explain that we wanted to sail at 0600 next morning and I was assured that there would be officials on duty at a quarter of an hour before that time to see that we could. We were also assured of a piece of paper to protect us from overzealous soldiers at Cnide, a coastal ruin on the way down to Rhodes which we specially wanted to visit next day. In fact, everything seemed fine.

Dutifully at 0545 next morning I visited the Customs office. The man on duty was asleep; after I had woken him, he asked me to 'sit down' in that infuriating way one meets in the timeless Levant, and wandered off to 'find Dad'. After half an hour or so I tracked him down to the souvenir store, where he was having coffee with the owner and his son. In a frenzy of irritation, I forced them to accompany me to the house, first of all of the harbour master, who signed some papers sleepily and dozed off again, and then to that of the chief of police. This gentleman had to be woken, his face washed and dragged down to the port, where a sort of reunion then took place (plenty of admonitions to me to 'sit down') while everyone chewed the cud over how to fill in the right forms to get rid of us. It seemed that during the night our passports had been mislaid in the souvenir store, thus adding fuel to the slow-burning flames of delay and bureaucracy. We at last got clearance at 0730, an hour and a half late. I must warn other yachts about visiting this port: the Crusader Castle of St Peter is very fine and, were it situated anywhere else in Turkey, I would think it more than worth a visit. But the port was so badly administered that every yacht I know of which has gone there has come away with nothing but complaints. Some of them have even determined never to call at a Turkish port again. A pity, because the natives are friendly and the harbour is about the best protected on this stretch of coast.*

At Cnide there are two ports, the north and the south. Each dating from ancient Greek times, they both nestle behind the shelter of Cape Krio on which there is a powerful and important light marking the southern entrance to the Cos Channel. The entry to the northern port, which is much the smaller, has silted, so we chose the southern. Here, too, one must take care of the sunken mole: on a normal summer's day it is clearly visible beneath the water. The anchorage is good.

There is a detachment of Turkish soldiers permanently stationed here. Their duties are not very clear, but there is a telephone in their little hut next to the southern port and so I imagine they are kept permanently on the 'qui vive' from their H.Q. We rowed ashore in the dinghy with mixed feelings, for others before us had told us of inhospitable receptions, sometimes enlivened by gunfire. Their leader advanced towards us menacingly, or so it seemed. 'Cigarettes?' he asked (the Turkish word is similar). We smiled and produced a few packets. The ice was broken: cordial relations had been established and for the rest of our visit the detachment wandered amiably round the ruins of Cnide with us. They were genuinely sorry to see us go, for it must be a dull life for them. We had meanwhile produced our magic paper from Bodrum—I do not know whether it had been read or not, for many Turks are illiterate—but we left it with them for good measure. The ruins of the once-important city of Cnide are not of first importance. It is the siting of the two harbours which has the most appeal.

And so a long lazy afternoon down the Turkish coast to the Greek island

---

* The recent appointment of a 'Director of Tourism' at Bodrum should go far towards bringing about an improvement.

of Rhodes, conveniently placed for watering and revictualling. Much shipping was passed on passage, for this is a main international lane northwards
from the Levant ports to the Dardanelles. Off Rhodes was anchored the
American naval auxiliary vessel *Courier*, which broadcast the 'Voice of
America' radio programme to the Near East and also off Rhodes harbour
were exercising two Greek destroyers, the *Navarino* and *Nike*, to whom we
dipped our ensign in salute. An hour before we had called Rhodes Radio
to announce our E.T.A. and been answered in perfect English. It was
refreshing, after the difficulties of getting into contact with Athens Radio,
surely the most inefficient radio station in all the Mediterranean, to find
that Rhodes and Iraklion (in Crete) replied almost at once to any call. I
learned later that Athens is so inoperative mainly because of its situation
radiophonically and that a new station much more easily accessible on the
air was very shortly to be built.

Among our old friends in the yachting world lying at Rhodes when we
arrived were the British *Mullion II*, *Carrina* (John Staniland) and the
German *Queen II* (formerly *Sintra*), who later, I hear, penetrated the
Bosphorus into the Black Sea. It was nice to be in Rhodes again, where I
had wintered a few years ago and where we had many old friends. The last
part of our journey still lay ahead.

'You are mad to go over to Turkey,' said our Greek friends in Rhodes.
I had heard this so often before that its impact was nil. In Turkey, too, they
said: 'You are fools to go to Greece.' It is a tragic situation. By getting
together, a vast trade, with consequent riches to both sides, could be
achieved, as it indeed used to be. But now, at best it could be called a
studied indifference, each side maligning and misrepresenting the other.
Both noses are cut off to spite both faces. A yachtsman must be careful not
to seem to take sides.

The Americans, in their good ship *Courier*, had supplied the port office
in Rhodes with a transcript of the Malta weather forecast for the sea area
'Jason', in which we found ourselves. This proved most valuable—the only
reliable one we had had for ages—and we decided to sail for the Turkish
port of Fethiye opposite, some 45 miles distant. There was a last-minute
scramble to get the passports stamped and, disdaining suggestions that
Marmarice—a Turkish port of entry rather closer than Fethiye—was
preferable, we cleared and sailed. It is very important to get one's passport

properly stamped when entering or leaving Greece. This prevents the accusation, when leaving next time, that one is not really there at all.

Passage over to Fethiye was uneventful until near the end, when one of the thunderstorms (with its associated high winds) that we had been warned of in the forecast broke loose. Our arrival in Fethiye was thus something of a drama, especially as I had foolishly forgotten to buy the detailed chart of the harbour approaches. The most important thing was to leave the red-lit buoy marking the edge of the harbour shoals to port, which we duly did. There was a convenient berth available alongside the little commercial quay and we thankfully grabbed it. The local officials were friendly and helpful, even going to the length of sending down a 'guide', who laboriously explained the wonders of his district to us in halting English. At the end of his lecture he handed us a slip of paper on which, to my surprise, the whole of his speech appeared in print. It was only then that I discovered that this sort of 'Press conference' which he had just given us represented the whole of his knowledge of the English language; further conversation was therefore impossible.

Though the whole of this area is now covered by the modern Turkish province of Mugla, its main interest to the visitor is that it was formerly the ancient kingdoms of Pamphylia and Lycia, inhabited by Hittite and other civilizations even before the Greeks settled there. We had heard a great deal about the celebrated Lycian tombs, great temples of death cut into the red rock faces, and were especially pleased to hear there were some at Fethiye.

Our 'guide' managed to get us a Land-Rover and off we set to visit the cliffs. The outcome was impressive. The Lycian tombs were vast affairs, inevitably desecrated and rifled during the Byzantine era, but still majestic in their size and their spurning of the time that passed them by. We had meant to continue to the ruins of Xanthus, former capital of this area, but the Land-Rover broke down. I tried to change some Greek money at the bank, but was told it was politically unacceptable. The modern town of Fethiye is quite without interest, though here and there the ruins of Telmessus, as it was called in Greek times, are visible. As a port of refuge, however, it is superb, the bay being able to accommodate very large vessels. This, with the fact that it is well administered and friendly, make me place it high on the list of ports to be visited.

We decided to sail on southwards without seeing Xanthus. This was a grave error, for it was perfectly clear to us later on that taxis were unobtainable at all other local ports and the inland sights were thus barred to us, unless we were lucky enough to scrounge a lift on a camel train, which we gathered was extremely uncomfortable.

Henry Denham recommends the island of Gemili, outside Fethiye, as a yacht anchorage, and we were pleased with his advice. Not only was it well protected and the water delightfully clear, but adjacent lay the fabulous ruins of what I imagined must be an entire Byzantine or Venetian city, covering the whole island with towers, gates and churches sprouting up like flowers among the green shrubbery. What is this place? I could find no mention of it in any guide book. No one has ever heard of it. This coast will be full of these surprises and conundrums till someone starts to document and explain it. Truly we were on the edges of beyond.

The coast southwards of Fethiye is steep and rugged, with high mountains inland. It is known as the Seven Capes, and the west wind, which blows so strongly in the Rhodes Channel, here seems to die slowly as one ploughs one's way westwards. Ashore, we could see the ruins of ancient Patara, whence St Paul set sail for Caesarea. Nowadays the city is almost completely covered by the sands swept over it by winter gales. Offshore, one notices swirls of dirty water sent up by the River Xanthus, which forces its way out from beneath the sea bed.

The Turks had advised us to spend the night at Kalkan, in the Bay of Kalamaki. On inspection, however, it turned out to be very badly protected. Three Turkish tugs lay off it, pitching and rolling heavily. Badly put off, we made for a more protected spot close into the north-western corner of the bay, put a line ashore and spent a quiet night. The Admiralty chart showed a great depth right close in, but, as is so often the case, the bottom shelved steeply and we were able to find anchorage in 5 fathoms about 50 yards offshore. A Turkish coaster joined us during the night. As in other deserted Turkish anchorages, we were in no way disturbed by anybody.

Dawn broke serene and, after a swim around our vessel, we set sail again eastwards through the Archipelago north of and surrounding the island of Castelorizzo, the last outpost of Greece off this Turkish mainland. I was not at all clear of the nationality of some of these rocks and islets, but I do not suppose it mattered much. What did matter was to make sure that one was where one thought one was and for the first time for weeks I found myself anxiously glued to the chart. We were bound for the small Turkish port of Kaş (formerly the Greek Andiphilo).

Around a headland, Kaş eventually hove into sight. It looked more Greek than Turkish, even its mosque being a converted Byzantine-type church, and many of its houses still painted white, as they were in Greek times. The entrance to its tiny harbour is difficult to find, as one has to be able to distinguish the seaward end of a sunken mole. Even when once inside the mole, especially if there is any westerly sea, there is not very good protection, and we lunched in some danger of the *salade niçoise* sousing our decks in oil. The Turks seemed amused by our arrival, but none did anything about us until we rowed ashore. Here we were greeted by a formidable array of officials, each anxious to entertain us with coffee, Turkish cigarettes and lemonade. To hurry was useless and we resigned ourselves to an hour or more of clearance inward, to be rewarded with a conducted tour of the very well-preserved Greek theatre on top of the hill. Like many Greek theatres, it looks westwards towards the setting sun—in this case out to sea—so that the afternoon performances took place against a sunset backcloth, with the sea and the islands beyond.

It was not easy to get away from Kaş, so friendly were its people. I have since been in correspondence with the port officials and sent them photographs and had grateful letters in return. The harbour master, on learning that our next port was to be the Greek island of Castelorizzo opposite, said: 'Please give our best regards to Jannis, the harbour master there.' 'But why not go over yourself one day?' A shrug of the shoulders. I had suggested the impossible. So do politics poison human relations.

With 'Q' and the Greek courtesy flag once again flying we ended our half-hour crossing from Kaş to the pretty and well-protected port of Castelorizzo. Everyone was delighted to see us. They get mighty few visitors, the lifeline being the weekly steamer to Rhodes. There was a yacht station (duty-free fuel available, but not fresh water). The only fresh water was stored in Arab-built tanks high up on the island and does not look up to much. The town was once prosperous (you can tell this was so from the lovely architecture of its old palazzos) and was a great trading centre between Egypt and the Dardanelles. During the war the Germans held it and the British bombed it. It is largely in ruins today, the 400 or 500 pathetic inhabitants being more or less paid to stay there by the Greek Government, who are unanxious for it and the adjacent islets to be annexed by Turkey. There is nothing to do but fish and drink 'ouzo'; this the locals do with a vengeance.

Castellorizzo (from the Italian Castello Rosso—Red Castle, from the colour of its cliffs) nevertheless boasts one Lycian tomb and the most magnificent 'Blue Grotto' type of semi-submarine grotto I have ever seen. Beside it the celebrated Blue Grotto of Capri is nothing at all. Yet it is mentioned on no tourist literature—no guide-book knows of it. We were taken to it in a local fishing-boat. She stopped off it and we transhipped into a rowing-boat which, ourselves ducking to avoid the grotto ceiling, rushed us perilously through the waves until we were inside it. We were in a vast blue cathedral, silent but for the distant ocean, a strange pale-blue light from the sea-bed shining upwards into the vault. I shall never forget it.

Next day I went for a long walk around the island alone. The place compels solitude; it has so much to say to so few people. Here much of the famous film *The Guns of Navarone* was made and the locals are proud to have played 'bit' parts in it. On a small plateau are the cisterns, now sadly decayed, where the island's sparse water is stored. Adjacent are some ruined Cyclopean walls, evidence of early civilization. Several huge churches dominate the town and there is a disused mosque at the end of the quay. I would like to be the owner of one of the lovely houses now falling to bits: I imagine a fiver would secure. At evening a few lights flicker, a dog barks, a guitar strikes up at a taverna near the quay. By 10 o'clock Castelorizzo is sleeping fitfully, wondering what the morrow will bring.

It was time to go back to Rhodes and civilization. It is 70 miles of sometimes stormy water, so a forecast is nice to have. As I half-feared, the telephone was not working and the hills surrounding the port made it impossible to use my R/T. But the sea did not look all that bad and there was always a Turkish port or two to put into if things did go wrong. So we sailed, with half the population lending a hand. It was a bit tricky getting through the Castelorizzo Archipelago close to last light, but we made it. The wind, which was around Force 4, died gradually and the spray at my bows dropped accordingly. *September Tide* was saying farewell to Turkey— or was it 'au revoir'?

6
Turkey Revisited

Some old haunts and many new ones
get checked and brought up to date

Sick of the Cyclades, bored by the Bosphorus and generally allergic to the Aegean and all its works, I was glad to base myself most of summer 1965 on Rhodes, that pearl among Dodecanese islands.

It was with relief that I contemplated the calm possibilities of Turkey's western coastline—Anatolia to the initiated, from the ancient Greek word *anatole*, meaning eastwards. I had had a fair crossing—mostly by starlit night—from my winter base at Piraeus. To me, the standard tourist traps of Mykonos, Delos and Patmos had just been flashing white lights of varying characteristics and intensity. And now I was in Rhodes, with the mountains of Turkey only 10 miles across the Rhodes Channel.

There was plenty to do before my guests arrived. Captain Kipriotis, probably the most efficient harbour master Rhodes has ever boasted, had to be visited and questioned about the tragic loss at his harbour precincts of Bobby Somerset's *Trenchemer*. I could not resist the old jibe that a starboard-hand light at the entry to Mandraki yacht harbour would have prevented such a happening. Kipriotis was adamant. 'True, it would help anyone approaching from north-west. We used to have one marking the submerged moles there, but the gales carried it away.' 'Why didn't you put it back again?' 'It would have been lost in the next gale. And anyway, too many lights are a bad thing. A ship approaching from south-east has no trouble making Mandraki by keeping the big light to port.' But *Trenchemer* was approaching at right-angles.' 'Then he should have hugged the lighthouse.' No good arguing. Personally, I am convinced there is a

Bodrum (Halicarnassus)
Black Is.
Orak Is.
Sehir Is.
(Cleopatra Is.)
Seven Islands
Marmarice
Karagac Bay
KOS
Gulf of Kos
(Kerme Korfezi)
Datça
Yilancik Is.
Dalyar
C. Krio
Sam Is.
Hisaronü Korfezi
Ciftlik Bay
Ekinciks Cove
Baba Is.
Cnide
Nemos Is.
Nar Is.
Mesudiyeh Cove
Khondra Is.
Kizil Is.
Peskime
Miliontes Bay
Simi
Port Sertche
SIMI
Panormitis Bay
Seskli Is.
Loryma Bay
Trombeto Is.
C. Aloti
Rhodes Town
KHALKL
Alinia
RHODES
Aege
Lindas
S

13. The

Köycegiz

cöz
Kocek

Kizil Is.
Is.
Fethiye
Yorgun Köyu
Gemili Is.

TURKEY

Antalya

Gulf of Antalya

Phaselis
Tekrova

Chimaera

Cirali Cove
Cineviz
Cove

River Xanthus

Xanthus
Patara
Kalkan

Seven Capes

Myra
Yali Anchorage
Kas

Finike

Gulf of Finike

Myra Pt.
Gökkaya Is.
Kekova Is.

Sulu Is.
C. Gelidonya

Çatal Is.
Ufak Is.
St. Georges Is.
Castellorizo Is.

Blue
Grotto

Ic Is.
Ipsili Is.

Anatolia

strong case for a starboard-hand light here and would gladly subscribe to
have one installed.

Rhodes is a good place for shopping. You can get Schweppes tonic water
(the only place I know of in Greece) at the outrageous price of 2s. 6d. a
bottle (split). Greek tonic water being undrinkable, this is something to
know. All spirits are very reasonable—being far cheaper than in England.
The same applies to cigarettes and liqueurs and the grocers' shops are like
Fortnum and Masons. Curiously, there is not a ship chandler within sight
and technicians are hard to come by. I always use the fellows from the
Rhodes Municipal Technical School to see to my engine repairs and so on.
They are always friendly, quick on the scene and make no attempt to
overcharge—rather a change after Piraeus. Rhodes is indeed a place to
linger: the only real disadvantage to the yachtsman is the atrocious noise
along the quayside during the night hours, when all the drunks of the island
seem to compete with St Tropez to make the night hideous for the water-
borne. The Greeks are trying to make Rhodes a yachting centre and they
know that this is one of the chief snags. The unfortunate placing of the
town sewer might also be mentioned, but let us not look this Rhodian gift-
horse too closely in the mouth.

Two Turkish trips from Rhodes as a base were uppermost in my mind.
I wanted first to do a grand sweep along the whole coast between Finike
(this side of the redoubtable Cape Gelidonya) and Ephesus and so back to
base. Fresh from this triumph, I proposed to take it easier on the next leg
and potter into some of the places I had known before and do a little fishing
in the more remote bays that a yacht has probably never visited. On both
of these cruises I would be deeply interested to know to what extent those
wicked and terrible Turks might have mended their ways. The Turkish
Tourism Directorate in London had assured me that a cry had gone out in
the Anatolian wilderness that we were coming. Had it done any good?

It was 7 o'clock in the forenoon on June 30 when we slipped quietly out
of Mandraki and set course 105 for the minute island of Castellorizzo,
Greece's most easterly possession, barely 2 miles from the Turkish mainland. It was a superb day, with a light following wind and the shade
temperature in my wheelhouse was soon well above the 100° Fahrenheit
mark. On deck we could only survive by drenching ourselves with sea-
water from the deck-wash hose. The Turkish mountains of the Seven

Capes soon hove in sight and from then onwards past Catal Island and the several islets encumbering the westerly approaches to Castellorizzo, we were never far from the land. In the great heat that still enveloped us at tea-time, it was a relief to have a swim at anchor in the rock-strewn approaches before entering Castellorizzo harbour. We had cleared out of Greece at Rhodes and had our passports stamped as leaving the country, a necessary precaution, for at Castellorizzo there are no such facilities—if you find yourself there and wanting to go to Kaş in Turkey, which you can see across the water, you are obliged to go all the way back to Rhodes for clearance.

A quiet night among the Australian accents of former Castellorizzians come back to see how the island is faring, a few gallons of fuel shipped (for who knew when we could expect to see more?) and even a little fresh water (by buckets from wells in people's houses—sparingly given) and, having duly risked our necks getting in and out of the island's superb Blue Grotto, we made the half-hour trip over to Kaş, the Crescent replacing the Cross at my courtesy yard.

Clearing into Turkey can be a cumbersome process, but here we were among old friends and things went quickly and smoothly. The little town is pretty at a distance, but very poor indeed as far as supplies are concerned. Bread and a few tomatoes are about all one can rely on finding. There is no ice and, there being no quay to go alongside, one cannot easily avail oneself of the plentiful water. We walked up to the superb ancient Greek theatre, made a note of the Lycian tomb in the village street and turned in early.

None of us will ever forget the next day. The 2-hour coastal trip along the mainland until one enters Kekova fjord to the east is pretty enough, but the placid waters of Kekova, watched over by a dream-like Crusader castle and rimmed by many cables of ghostly ruins along deep estuaries and up narrow creeks have to be seen to be believed. The Admiralty Chart 241 is vital for this excursion, but as it has not been brought up to date since Captain Beaufort (of wind-scale fame) surveyed this distant coast in the early nineteenth century, one must treat it with caution. However, I found no trouble in sighting the main westerly entrance to the sound, with its white markings on the rocks, nor in making my approach to the castle anchorage, though locating the shoal off the western end of Kekova Island itself did give us a little thought, as did the entrance to Yali anchorage, where we spent the day. Returning to the Crusader castle late that afternoon and going ashore, we found it too dark to shift berth in these unlit waters when we got back aboard, so we spent the night there, watched by silent groups of Turkish peasants in rowing-boats (what the Queen Mother, I believe, has described as 'a Zoo dinner', when one feels like an animal in a cage at feeding-time) and later savagely attacked by mosquitoes against which we had no defences. Please note: if sailing anywhere east of Rhodes in mid-June to early September, remember the mosquitoes and, if possible, see that your ports are gauzed.

From Kekova coastwise eastwards is fascinating. On leaving the fjord, one comes out into a bay, on the eastern side of which a brackish river runs out into the sea, past some ruins which mark the site of the ancient port of Myra, where St Paul changed ships on his last voyage to his trial in Rome. Farther along the coast, which is notable for its sand-dunes, one can see inland the extensive ruins of the old town of Myra itself and the far-flung necropolis adjacent. Sand-dunes give way to reddish-brown cliffs and soon the little town of Finike comes into sight, the seas calming as one rounds the several capes.

Next time I have lunch with Henry Denham, I am going to make him pay the bill. His excellent book *The Eastern Mediterranean*, which was my Bible all last summer, speaks of 'an inner boat harbour recently constructed (at Finike) which is a great help for yachts'. Heading towards this yachtsman's boon like a hacking-horse to its stable, I was dismayed to find myself aground on one of the dangerous rocks at the river entrance also mentioned. We were even more surprised, when we went ashore and peered into every possible place in the town, that the boat harbour did not, in fact, exist. Worse was to come when we tried to go stern to the quay, for the current of ice-cold water from the river brought my bows over to such an extent that I finally gave up the task. The only way to berth in Finike, I am certain, is to anchor off the river and let your stern swing seaward.

Finike itself is not up to much. But it has the great advantage that its authorities give no trouble and that ice, as well as fruit and vegetables, can easily be obtained. There is also fresh water, but the tap is well away from the quay. The anchorage is good holding. It is a convenient place for visiting the ruins of Myra, about an hour in a taxi, costing some £3 or £4.

There are banks, which change dollars at a net rate of 8.80 Turkish lire to the dollar, whereas the free-market rate is about 11. (Beware of free-market dealings, which are illegal and simply not worth while, but you may legally import up to 200 lire in Turkish notes per person and sometimes you can get these abroad at free-market rates.)

Enough of this eastwards going. We put about from Finike and—once more traversing the fairy realms of Kekova, made the long hop to Fethiye, one of the best Turkish ports for watering and provisioning and where the authorities are unusually helpful. Tersane island, near Fethiye, with its enclosed harbour among the ruins of a former Greek colony and a few sponge-diving vessels, gave shelter for a night. It was then only a short hop to Dalyan Island, off the mouth of the River Koycegiz, which leads up to the spectacular ruins of ancient Caunus, visible indeed some way seaward. This part of the world has so few navigable rivers that we were delighted to be able to anchor in the lee of the island, launch the dinghy and motor some miles up the river to Caunus itself and the modern Turkish village that surrounds it. It was not difficult to enter the river: there was, indeed, a bar, but the western side of the river mouth was relatively unencumbered and I would say there was about 2 fathoms of water there. In fact, on a calmer day, I would have been prepared to take my yacht into the river and make the fascinating ascent through the reeds. A Turkish outpost dealt with our papers politely: this is a trip I can confidently recommend. On returning to the yacht, we found the afternoon wind had risen and those still aboard were having an uncomfortable time. Navigation in this part of the world should, as elsewhere in this general area, be confined to the morning hours where possible.

Dalyan Island is useless as a night anchorage, so we shifted berth to Ekincik Cove a few miles north-west, where one can expect to find shelter in almost any weather. Nevertheless, even here it is wise to lay out two anchors if staying the night, as sudden gusts from the high land occur even in summer.

Still westwards from here, it is a pity to miss Marmarice, at the head of a deep and attractive fjord. The pretty little Greek-Genoese village is becoming important as the Turkish end of the run to Rhodes, much patronized by tourists in season, but the harbour authorities still have a lot to learn from places like Fethiye and Finike. Lately a fresh water terminal to the quay was completed and we also managed to get ice—that essential of happy cruising in these waters. There was a modern hotel crammed with assorted international tourists and a competent agent, educated, to my surprise, at an American university.

Between Marmarice and the gulf of Symi, there are a number of excellent anchorages. We chose Loryma for lunch, where the chart mentions 'extensive ruins' and indeed it is correct. The whole of this coastline is studded with antiquities not mentioned in any guide-book and will one day be a paradise for yachtsmen and antiquarians alike. With the summer north-west winds gusting down these bays, one has to beware of one's anchor dragging.

The shortest route from this coast to Datça, the next Turkish port, is through the Nimos Passage (about 50 yards wide and with about 2 fathoms in the fairway) to the north of the islands forming the Symi group. There is no need to go ashore or observe any formalities in doing so, with the exception of changing one's courtesy flag from Turkish to Greek. Symi is a lovely island, though its people are leaving it. Recently, an American church organization gave it a plant to make fresh water from sea water: I slipped there once—very primitive but very effective—at a fee of Drs. 2,000 (about £23) which is Drs. 1,000 less than in Piraeus.

The winds are so strong at Datça that the only safe berth is with an anchor out and stern lines to the shore. There is plenty of water close in and the locals are extremely helpful in giving a hand, so one need have no fears in going there. They like to clear you into Turkey here, but have little experience, and when one gets to the next port there is often found to be some vital paper or other missing, so one must expect complications. Adjacent is the magnificent bay of Miliontes, where I have had some of the best fishing ever. The Turks are not a maritime people and fish their coasts but rarely, so conditions in the fish world get rather overcrowded.

A short stop for lunch at Cnide (Cape Krio) to look at the ruins and exchange cigarettes with the Turkish military outpost (now thoroughly used to the yachtsmen they used formerly to shoot at) before grudgingly entering Bodrum, that bane of all peaceful yachtsmen. I found the port little changed, I am sorry to say. The authorities do everything in their power to ensure that a yacht has a horrible time, even to the extent of playing you into the hands of an inefficient and expensive agent. This is the

only port in the world at which I have been asked to pay light dues as well
as harbour and sanitary dues, even though I only went out on a day trip,
and where one is charged extra for sailing on Sundays or after Customs
hours. I have not met one single yacht—even a Turkish yacht—which did
not have unpleasant memories of this place. *Clonsilla*, the Guinness family's
yacht, was asked £25 sterling for anchoring off Bodrum in 1965—simply,
one imagines, because the locals wished to enrich themselves. I have
promised to do what I can to help this situation by complaining to the
Turkish Tourist Board in London. Bodrum excuses itself by saying that
smuggling goes on here on a large scale: it makes no attempt, however, to
distinguish between the law-abiding tourist and the obvious contraband
boat. A ray of hope is shed on this unhappy port by the recent appointment
of an educated and intelligent Director of Tourism to the municipality. I
wish him well.

There are endless places to stop at between Bodrum and Kuş Adasi, port
for Ephesus, but we only made two of them, Myndus, and an inlet near
Point Kyriaki, just south of the sensational ruins of Didymus. Both were
enchanting and we were not troubled by anyone.

It was a joy to be at Kuş Adasi again and be looked after by the excellent
Monsieur Sumer of the Akdeniz Agency. The newly built boat harbour is
a bit small for some of the M.L. type yachts that seem to want to use it
these days. They should really berth at the steamer quay, where they can
go alongside and where fresh water is laid on. We watered from the town
fire brigade's tanker. Ice was plentiful as well as good fresh provisions,
including some of the best steak I have ever eaten. Turkish meat is notably
good and is, I hear, smuggled over to Greece a great deal, where it is in
short supply. On passage northwards I had passed Eric Williams, the
author, in his *Escaper* sailing southwards on a reciprocal course.

And so back to Samos, Patmos, Kalymnos, Cos and to Rhodes, happy to
be with our Greek friends. Fran, our cook, was especially pleased to be able
to get to the shops in Cos and Rhodes, for, whichever way one looks at it,
the Greek way of life is considerably more *évolué* than the Turkish.

It only remained for us, on our next local cruise, to add to the laurels of
the previous trip by exploring the Gulf of Kos. I had always wanted to do
this. We had heard great things about it from the agency in Marmarice
and our friends who ran the excellent hotel at Bodrum, an emancipated

couple whose views one could rely on, had sung its praises loudly. We were
not disappointed.

There are several delightful and picturesque anchorages towards the
head of the Gulf of Kos, or the Kerme Korfezi as it is known in Turkish.
The Admiralty Chart 'Plans in Kerme Korfezi' shows them all clearly. It
would indeed be difficult to find a good reason for giving these remote
places in such detail, were it not for the fact that during the last war the
British used them extensively for harbouring their coastal forces directed
against the German- and Italian-held Greek islands. The anchorages most
used were Yedi Adalari (Seven Islands), the Sehir Islands (where legend
has it that Antony and Cleopatra spent part of their honeymoon) and the
inlet known as the Bay of Degirmen, with the adjacent Kahya islands. Had
time allowed, I would have welcomed a visit to all three, but as it was, we
only managed to get to the Seven Islands. Inside these there is yet another
sheltered creek, and with this as a base we dinghied around each day,
reaping a rich harvest from the sea. The place is quite deserted and the
pines cool their parched roots in the dark waters of the myriad creeks—a
place where you are close to the basis of things.

Were this chapter twice as long, I would tell you, too, of Yorgun Koyu,
near Fethiye, the prettiest anchorage I have ever lain in, of Baba Island
near Marmarice, of Çiftlik Bay opposite Rhodes, where we had some of the
best fishing ever, of Mesudiye Cove, of Porto Sertcheh, of Guirejik Island
off Bodrum, of Palmuet Bay and Tuerk Bueku. And are not the rest of the
places in this Turkish heaven in the Book of the Admiralty Mediterranean
Pilot?

But all need not be utter stillness in Turkey. The people know how to
enjoy themselves, as we discovered at a little port called Guelluek in the
Bight of Mandalya just north of Bodrum on this trip. Strolling ashore after
dinner, we found ourselves button-holed into attending the festivities in the
local restaurant. A string and percussion band (mostly strange wooden
instruments) was playing. The men were sitting around in the middle of
things, respectfully watched by their womenfolk from a distance. I was
about to exhibit my cavalier Westernism by inviting a lady to dance, when
I was reminded that it was not customary here for them to join in such
public displays. To my embarrassment, I then learned that I was expected
to entertain the locals by doing some sort of *pas seul*, 'à la grécque'. It is

churlish to refuse, so my nanny used to tell me, with the result that I soon found myself performing an amazing series of steps to the claps and cheers of the locals. My crew were, of course, obliged to join in, after which the harbour master and his assistants gave a few spirited renderings before the evening drew to a close in a cloud of *raki*-induced good humour. Anglo-Turkish relations had, we felt, been closely cemented.

7

Landfall in the Levant

Cyprus—The Lebanon—Syria
and the fabulous South Coast of Turkey
'where no one ever goes'

One of my life's ambitions was realized on September 2, 1965. For at 0630 that day I sailed *September Tide* from Rhodes on a six weeks' cruise to the Levant and Cyprus. One cannot undertake a 1,500-mile cruise—even in the Mediterranean—without a certain amount of thought. From a glance at the records, it is obvious that the winds in September in the area between Rhodes and Cyprus are west to north-westerly, that the sea area east of Cyprus is subject to light variables, with south-west predominating, and that up the Levant coast, south to south-west prevails. The southern coast of Turkey generally experiences settled weather, the daytime onshore breezes giving way to land breezes at night. Added to this, the existence of a north- and west-going clockwise current along the shores of the Levant countries and southern Turkey confers another advantage on someone intending this voyage at this time. All in all, September seemed the ideal month.

And so it proved. All the way to Castellorizzo, where we stopped to fuel, the west-north-west winds gave us their following benediction. We completed the 70-sea-mile passage in just under 10 hours. The little port was much as it had been on our earlier visits this season, with the exception of the important news that a team prospecting for fresh water up by the original rain-water cisterns had claimed to have found its goal. If this proves to be true, one can see a new future as a distinctive tourist resort opening out for this tragic atoll.

It is 27 hours' run for me from Castellorizzo to the only sizable port in northern Cyprus—Kyrenia. So there was no object gained in making an early start. After a leisurely breakfast, we bade farewell to the lonely out-post of officials that came to say good-bye and left Greek soil for the last time in six weeks. Setting course inside Ipsili Island (also Greek—there are, in fact, three or four Greek islands in the Castellorizzo complex), I made my point of departure from it to steer 105 T. for the next day and night.

Looking at the chart, one would expect to be out of sight of land for quite some time on this passage. This proved not to be so. The high moun-tains of the Turkish Taurus range were in sight until sunset of that day and the Cyprus Troodos range came into sight at 0300 next day at the first loom of daylight. The wind again blew benevolently, so that for the whole passage it remained fine on my starboard quarter, though not enough to make it worth while rigging the steadying sails. The sea was what meteoro-logists would have described as slight.

Everything was, in fact, perfect, except for a plague of flies that never left us all passage. How is it possible that flies can thus harass a vessel so far out at sea? They were certainly not the same flies all the time. Our con-stant battle with the modern weapons of insecticide saw to that. But each time the battlefield was black with their dead bodies a fresh wave turned in to the attack. At night, flying-fish flew aboard and landed helplessly on the quarter-deck, there to breath their last. The moon shone down on this quiet if macabre scene, while at our bow and in the wake the generous phosphorescence of these waters traced our way eastwards.

The first loom of day came at 0300 and first light at 0400, when the Cyprus mountains could clearly be seen just where they belonged. Soon afterwards, at about 0600, Cape Kormakiti, our landfall preceding sighting Kyrenia, came up, and we made this cape with its offlying shoals at 0850, when we altered course slightly to starboard to follow the Cypriot north coast. Soon, the familiar landmarks of Kyrenia itself started to appear— the Lusignan skyline of the overhanging hills, the Crusader Castle at the harbour entrance and even (shades of prewar old ladies!) the Dome Hotel. The delightful little port itself had been greatly improved since I was last there as a land-borne tourist. The seaward mole had been extended to run parallel with the shore, thus giving protection from all weathers and a light

(Fl.R. 5 sec. 18 ft Vis. 5 miles) placed on the end of the new mole (this awaits publication on charts). There is, however, very little water in this approach channel—and indeed in the whole port—and my sounder did not register more than 8 or 10 ft. Buoys mark the fairway. I see from my log that we passed the pierheads at exactly midday—which gave me a passage time of 27 hours to cover the 206 miles from Castellorizzo.

I was delighted to find my old friends Yanoula and Bill Wakefield at the quayside in their Silver-built *Mawingo*, ready as ever to give a hand with the rather complicated berthing which this picturesque harbour requires. One drops an anchor as far away as one dares and puts one's stern into the only possible berth for a visitor, over by the harbour office. I must confess to some disappointment, after the glowing accounts I had heard of Kyrenia as a yacht harbour, to find that, in addition to there being very little water and a number of obstructions at the yacht berth, that there was, in fact, no really practical means of getting ashore comfortably. When one takes into account that there is a local rise and fall in the tidal level of some 18 in., the picture is even gloomier. However, warned about the possibility of an onshore wind bearing down on my port beam, I laid out a kedge anchor, applied the topping lift to my perilously perched stern gangway, and went ashore to say 'Hullo' to Cyprus.

Any illusions we had had about perhaps not being welcome in this charming island by reason of our nationality were soon dispelled. The locals, Cypriots and British alike, could not have been kinder or more genuinely glad to see us. The island, which once had a thriving tourist trade, is now quite deserted by foreigners. We were, I suppose, the only tourists there! Hotels which once housed hundreds now stood empty. The coming of the United Nations forces must have been a godsend to these establishments, as the officers and men are bound to go somewhere for relaxation and in doing so at least go some way towards populating them. And they seemed to have plenty of money to spend.

We paid several visits to the capital—Nicosia—by road. This was not always easy. It is only a few miles over beautiful country and takes about 25 minutes by private car. But the intervening territory is held by Turkish Cypriot forces and there are restrictions on passing it. Greeks can apparently only get through by joining the convoy which U.N.O. organizes twice daily—heavily escorted—so that if you take a bus you can only either do

22. Bodrum. St Peter's Castle and the port.

23. *September Tide* in the Iraq Petroleum Company very private harbour at Banyas (Syria).

24. The harbour at
Antalya with the
'Fisherman's Mosque'
in the background.

this or take another service which goes by a longer route and takes hours to by-pass the Turkish area. I twice drove back and forth in a diplomatic car (passports to be shown) and once in a car which I had hired and where, by also showing my passport, I was allowed through at once. U.N.O. troops are everywhere, all apparently and understandably bored to tears, as indeed I felt everyone must be by this absurd situation.

The shopping in both Nicosia and in Kyrenia was excellent. The prices were only a fraction higher than in England and all our usual goods were available in immense quantities, far more readily and more cheaply, for instance, than in Greece. In fact, I found conditions in Cyprus happier for a yacht going shopping than in the traditionally prosperous Lebanon. I took advantage of this situation to have a new cooker installed in my galley and to buy a record-player for the saloon. In Kyrenia, we had a new wind-vane made (price £3. 10s.) and some important electrical work done for less than a fiver.

One cannot say that food in Cyprus is especially cheap, nor is it often very imaginative, but it is infinitely better than in Greece, and at the Harbour Club in Kyrenia, run by that staunch couple Judy and Roy Findlay, you eat as well as anywhere in London. It was also a great pleasure to meet that well-known yachting character Andreas Kariolou at Kyrenia, where he runs, amongst other things, the Hotel Hesperides. He probably knows the coast of Cyprus, as well as of southern Turkey opposite, as well as any man alive, and his advice and help were of the greatest value. I was assured to learn from him that the Kyrenia Municipality (of which, need I hardly say, he is a member) is doing its utmost to transform this charming little port into a real paradise for the smaller type of yacht. The whole of the quayside is to be dredged and built up into modern berths and all facilities are to be provided there for the small boat, in line with Cyprus's programme for encouraging tourism. Indeed, while we were there, a fresh-water connection was being connected right opposite our berth.

There is also to be a patent slip on the opposite side of the harbour. So there are reasonable prospects that one day Kyrenia will be a good wintering port, especially if mooring-buoys are put down to avoid anchor troubles.

While we were there we received a daily visit from one or two rather deadly-looking small gunboats, which we were told had recently been delivered to the Cypriots from Russia. The public were not allowed to approach their berth, nor to walk along the outer mole, which we understood to be mined against possible invasion from Turkey, nor to take photographs of these positions.

My log records—I think with accuracy—that when we finally left this delightful place on September 9 we had the calmest passage of the whole season as we followed the outline of the Cypriot north coast along to the anchorage off Cape Andreas for the night. Before sailing at 0700, I had carefully told the Kyrenia harbour master of our intentions, which I understood had to be known so that shore patrols might be expecting us. Part of this coast is Turkish held and subject to upheavals.

One cannot pretend that the coast is especially interesting. There are no harbours with the exception of a few deserted trading posts, and the Admiralty chart has the utmost difficulty in finding landmarks from which one can take one's bearings. Remarks like 'large rock' or 'tree' are furthermore of not much use to the navigator, as, especially when poorly lit, they are barely recognizable. We almost longed for gunfire to break the tedium of this lengthy day.

After what seemed an age, we caught sight of *Mawingo* anchored in one of the several inlets near Cape San Andreas. There are quite a few of these little places if one looks hard for them, and perhaps it would have been better for us if we, too, had used one of them (generally well sheltered at this season when the winds give little trouble, but useless in winter) instead of pressing on regardless. But I had told the Kyrenians that we would be stopping the night in the anchorage off the San Andreas monastery, so we pushed on. Always the prudent mariner, I resisted the idea of taking one of the several channels through the Khlides islands at the end of the mainland promontory, but rounded the whole group and altered south-west towards the monastery, which by then was in sight. I had shortly before this called up Cyprus Radio to see if they had any messages for us, but the intervening range of mountains (the station is unfortunately placed at Limassol) made communications so difficult that I abandoned the attempt. This later proved a tragedy, as they had a message for me from home which I would dearly have liked to receive. I wonder whether it would be possible for radio stations to advise ports in their area that they have something for a vessel, so that harbour masters could act as channels?

I chose the southerly of the two coves off San Andreas Monastery in which to spend the night and some friendly fishermen ferried me ashore to have a look at the monastery buildings. I found them quite uninteresting. My arrival precipitated something of a crisis, however, for the good people seemed to think I was some sort of an official come to make a check. This impression was heightened when I was back aboard having dinner, during which a boatload of armed police arrived and wanted to see our papers. I was a little surprised, after all my efforts to do the right thing on leaving Kyrenia, that our arrival had apparently not been noised abroad, especially when the police rather pathetically told me they had had to bicycle 14 miles from their village, but we mollified them with some cigarettes, some English books and some French brandy, so they left us quite happily.

As we were weighing for Famagusta at dawn next day, the two Russian-built gunboats we had seen in Kyrenia came roaring up and around us. But by now we were old friends and able to exchange waves. It is difficult to see what these two little craft can do against the comparative majesty of the Turkish fleet concentrated across the way, but I was told that they probably did a good job of frightening away illegal landings and so forth, at least on the stretch of coast they normally patrolled. At any rate, with their amazing speed and manoeuvrability, they were an added attraction to our visit.

The coastline between Cape San Andreas and Famagusta is flat and uninteresting and we decided, instead of following it, to make a direct passage across the 48 miles of intervening Mediterranean. Famagusta itself is flat and the port comes up quickly at the last moment, none of the so-called 'conspicuous' objects on the chart being visible until one is right on top of them. We did, however, make out the approach channel buoy in good time and on rounding it everything became as clear as day. The Polish-built outer harbour is now complete and the port was full of freighters of many nationalities. A Polish tug lingered on with some fifty men aboard checking the results of their labours.

As I had been told, I went alongside the commercial quay near the Port Office and cleared inwards. There is no system of 'yacht manifests' in

TURKEY

Perge · Aspendos
Side
Antalya
Phaselis
Bodrum   Marmarice   Cirali Cove
Xanthus Chimaera   Cineviz Cove
Kos   Fethiye Patara Myra
Nisiros   Simi   Kalkan   Finike
Tilos   Rhodes   Catal Is. Kas Kekova
Town   Kekova Castle
Rhodes

Karpathos

Mediterranean Se

Ayas
Mersin
Viransehir
(Soli)
Karatas
Iskenderun
Gulf of Iskenderun
Arsuz
Kizkalezi
Ayas
C. Fener
Tasucu
C. Resülhinzir
Seleucia
Orontes
Antioch
Narlic Cove
Ovacik
Dana Is.
Bay of Antioch
namur Castle
Gilindire
C. Bassite
amur
El Mina
Lattakia
Chlides Islands
Djeble
San Andreas
Monastery
Banyas
Banyas I.C.P. Harbour
Krak des
Chevaliers
makiti
Kyrenia
CYPRUS
Rouad
Tartous
Nicosia
Famagusta
Ramkine Is
Dhekelia
C. Greco
Tripole
Troodos
Mountains
Larnaca
Il Bourj
Bay
hos
Limassol
Byblos
C. Gata
Jouniyeh Bay
Beirut
Damascus
Sidon
Tyre
C. Carmel
Haifa
Tel Aviv

Levant

Cyprus as in Greece, Italy, Yugoslavia and so on, so one has to go through this cumbersome process at each port. The officials are, however, efficient and kind, so that not much time is wasted, and there is, of course, no language difficulty as everyone everywhere speaks English. Even my Greek seemed unintelligible to them (appalling pronunciation?). Here, they seemed particularly anxious to know if we were carrying firearms (for the other side?). With the exception of the isolated Turkish-held pockets on the north coast which we had passed the previous day without incident, the whole Cypriot coastline is Greek held.

Famagusta, although an excellent deep-water port for merchantmen, is not a good yacht harbour, as there are few berths where one can lie quietly. I had been careful to reconnoitre in advance and had managed to get the British Army's permission for us to lie at the quay bordering the so-called British Compound, a British 'reserved' territory inside the harbour complex. This has very recently been dredged, so that, although the dredging is not wide enough to allow berthing stern to the quay, a medium-sized yacht may by skilful manoeuvring nevertheless lie comfortably alongside. She must be wary of the considerable landing-craft traffic operated by the compound's bosses, the Royal Transport Corps, and there is also a rise and fall, as at Kyrenia, of about 18 in. daily to cope with, so that fenders need frequent adjustment. But one lies, quietly, safely and certainly in the best berth the town can offer.

Indeed, were I wintering now in Cyprus, I would prefer to do so in Famagusta rather than in the prettier, but less convenient, port of Kyrenia. There are certainly no other ports to choose from. Famagusta has good slipping facilities, water and fuel are easily obtainable, the shopping is excellent, the Army are most generous with their help, and there are lots of interesting shore excursions to be made. At the same time, the Cypriot harbour master's staff are very co-operative and you can buy most things you need for your boat. There is no actual yacht club, but the Royal Transport Corps maintain several medium-sized Army yachts in commission, which are almost constantly on charter to Levant ports and back by groups of enthusiastic soldiers—all clearly sailors *manqués*—who know a lot more about certain aspects of yachting than I do.

We thoroughly enjoyed our visit to Cyprus—despite the rather warlike atmosphere that occasionally made itself felt—and especially to Famagusta. With the aid of my good friend Barry Denny of the British High Commission at Nicosia, I signed on another crewman here, a soldier from a signals unit at Episkopi, Paddy by name, who was of the very greatest value aboard. The island is full of keen military and Air Force types who are members of the local sailing clubs and everybody was anxious to see that we had an enjoyable stay.

'Thither came Phoenicians, men famed for their ships, greedy knaves, bringing countless trinkets in their black ships . . .' The words of the *Odyssey* came whispering back to me over the years when, a small boy in a blue coat, grey trousers and a curious straw hat, I had sat listening with many others as our Greek master—tired but relentless—drove home Homer's immortal words to us.

We had slipped from Famagusta that evening at 1800, dined in the lee of Cape Greco and continued on a south-easterly course towards Beirut, some 110 miles away. Around 2100 we sighted and hailed the Army sailing yacht *Goldammer* outward bound from Famagusta to Beirut with an Army crew for a week's sailing leave. Alone on watch, I was left with my thoughts for company. The usual south-west swell struck us as we left the shelter of Cape Greco, but later this gave way to a calm: mindful of the north-going current running up the Levant coast, I had set a course which put us a mile or two south of Cape Beirut itself. What welcome awaited us in the first Arab country to which I had ever yachted?

About 0500, the Lebanese mountains began to show up to port with the waxing daylight, only to disappear later as the sun climbed his course. The sea was smooth, with a slight residual swell, when through the morning mists the outline of Cape Beirut and the great city came in sight. Beirut harbour lies a short way north of the cape, so we altered course and cruised along the foreshore, the city resplendent with its skyscrapers and modern apartment blocks edging past us in a slow panorama.

At precisely 1015 we passed through the pierheads of the outer harbour and saluted U.S.S. *Springfield*, flagship of the American Admiral Sixth Fleet, without getting an acknowledgement. United States warships are particularly bad at courtesies of this kind: I am glad to say that European warships are extremely punctilious. Beirut does not offer much to a yacht: the port is crowded with commercial shipping and the water is consequently none too clean or quiet. But the enterprising Beirut Yacht Club has taken over premises on the outer mole formerly housing a lighthouse and they do their best against fearful odds. Indeed, they at once sent out a launch to greet us and we were soon comfortably moored on two club buoys with the club secretary, Jean-Pierre Selwan, aboard explaining local drill to us.

Though the water was dirty, at least the berth was quiet and we felt reasonably secure from thieves. Fresh water was obtained from a metal tube which ran the length of the adjacent quay and thence by hose slung across to the buoys. Unless you watered at 0600 each day, you got hot to boiling water from it, as the heat of the sun increased.

Getting ashore was a real problem. First, one had to row oneself to the club landing some 100 yards away. Here one waited for the club ferry which plied at fairly regular intervals between 0700 and 1900. If you missed the last boat, you had had it. There was nothing to do but go down on one's knees to a local boatman, if one could be hailed, and pay him whatever he asked, which was always excessive. Coming back aboard at night was even more hazardous. First, one would have to endure the ignominies that one had already suffered from the port guards on one's way out, but in reverse. Only one distant gate was open. A boat could seldom be found for hours: the usual bargaining then ensued, it finally costing about 7s. 6d. to get to the club and row oneself exhaustedly back to the yacht.

Beirut harbour formalities had to be suffered to be believed. Customs, harbour master, health and immigration were each in separate buildings and in all one was expected to wait for some time before being attended to. Hearing that I had come from foreign with bonded stores, the Customs told me they were coming aboard to seal me, but they never did. I learned afterwards this was what they usually told yachtsmen, so that one's constant fear of their impending visit should prevent one from the smuggling that seemed inevitably expected of one. Of all the ports I have ever visited, I would place Beirut at the bottom of the list for yachting facilities.

I tried to get some repairs done to my outboard motor, but due to the lack of spares this was impossible. It was equally out of the question to find a ship chandler, but we did manage to locate a very good grocery where English things could be bought.

25. The anchorage off
Kekova Castle showing
the boat harbour built
of the local ruins by
the peasants.

26. Turkish fisherman
selling us their wares
at Kazakli.

27. The sea fortress known as the
'Maiden's Castle' is one of two castles
built by the Armenian kings at Kiskalezi.

The Yacht Club itself was the one bright spot in this wilderness of graft and muddle. The small clubhouse in the lighthouse with its fine view of all that went on in the port was charming, and Jean-Pierre and the others were all out to help, though I must admit that tipping the boatmen was rather an endless procedure. I gave the club a Red Ensign to fly as a courtesy to visiting British yachts, but I did not see it hoisted during our stay. Curiously enough, the club daily flew the flag of the Royal Yachting Association. I also gave a Red Ensign to a locally owned but British-registered motor yacht which said they were unobtainable in Beirut. As an afterthought, I gave a couple of my club burgees to the club, but they had none of theirs available for me. However, I took it out of them in Coca-Colas.

We did not much care for the city of Beirut, with its luxury side by side with utter squalor. The only thing that really amused us was that the ladies of what I believe is known as 'easy virtue' had their names up in neon lights outside their places of business. Food was very good, but extremely expensive. In fact, whatever one did really cleaned one out of all one's loose cash and one had the uncomfortable feeling that one should have paid more and tipped more, no matter how much one gave. 'Greedy knaves . . .'? Maybe the Phoenicians had not altered.

Unpleasant as Beirut itself is for a yachtsman, there are some superb excursions by road to be made locally. I shall never regret having visited Baalbek, and the endless formalities I had to endure to get to and from Damascus in Syria were well worth while. Unless going inland to Syria, it is as well not to bother to get a Lebanese or Syrian visa (normally obligatory for us) in advance. The local authorities issue a permit to circulate in the port area without a visa and this is usually quite enough. Besides, it costs nothing.

The club had warned us not to try to enter the picturesque harbour of Byblos, as there was insufficient water for us, so we coasted along as far as Juniyeh Bay, where I understand the enterprising Beirut Yacht Club is due to open a large 'Marina' next year, and thence shaped course for Tripoli. It had taken me 2½ hours to go through the Beirut departure formalities, so I was looking forward to a rest at sea and thanks to the expected following wind, this was forthcoming. The *Springfield*, too, had acknowledged my salute on leaving, so things were looking up. I wondered whether the

American Ambassador to Cyprus, Bill Belcher, who had just sailed over to visit the Admiral in the yacht *Copper Queen* from Limassol, had had something to do with it.

It was lunch-time when we got to Il Huri Bay, where often there is good anchorage. But the swell was coming around the point and we decided to press on, not lunching until we anchored off Tripoli itself, after a passage through the Sanina Strait, whose many islands shelter the port from southwest. At a wooden pier in the inner part of Tripoli harbour we eventually put our stern to the quay and welcomed the local officials aboard. In sharp contrast to Beirut, they were very nice and most efficient. This time the incantation 'Welcome to Lebanon' really seemed sincere. The works on the inner harbour have recently been finished by an Italian company and the shelter is good. I had a visit from a gentleman describing himself as a ship chandler with a letter purporting to be on the ship's notepaper of *Deianeira* R.Y.S., and signed 'Field Marchall [*sic*] Alexander, Lord of Tunis' recommending his services. Lord Astor would have laughed. We declined his services and engaged an English-speaking student to help us shop.

Next day we toured the town (I was fascinated to find a giant Turkish bath—formerly the Christian church of St Nicholas—with 'Behold the Lamb of God' still engraved on its somewhat dingy entrance) and then went off in a taxi, still with our guide, to see Byblos, probably the most ancient inhabited city in the world, whence the word 'bible' originates. Its city complex and diminutive harbour are quite unique. From a close inspection of the port, I formed the view that we could, after all, have got in, though whether we would have found a berth at its congested quay is another matter. I cannot really recommend the risk to other yachtsmen. There is now a light on the starboard-hand approach. I inquired the depth at the quays and was told 2 fathoms to starboard on entering, with rather less to port, where I noted some obstructions. On a calm day, I think the place justifies the hazard of an entry.

It was a trifle disconcerting to note that, while I was wandering around the port, my chauffeur and crew had been arrested by an infuriated Lebanese gentleman describing himself as 'Chief of Protocol' of the Lebanese Ministry of Information for being in possession of cameras without an official permit. This person and I then had quite a set-to, from which it emerged that, according to what he told me, permits were required for all foreigners taking photographs in Lebanon, an assertion which I simply don't believe. Interspersing his remarks with the standard phrase 'Welcome to Lebanon', he continued to say that Byblos was a military port, and therefore it was all the more necessary to have a permit to take photographs there. After an icy exchange of addresses, the interview came to an end. 'Welcome to Lebanon.' This incident was all the more surprising since I have always noted that the Lebanese take great trouble to get tourists to visit their expensive but interesting country.

On getting back to Tripoli, I inquired whether there was any truth in the matter of the photographic permit or not and was told by the police that they had never heard of such a regulation. When I came out of the police office a furious scene was going on between our Lebanese guide and a representative of the ship chandler with whom, as it turned out, we had not dealt. The Arabs are a very sensitive and jealous people and one has to be careful how one treats them, as it seems very easy to give offence. I started preparations for sailing early next morning: the Lebanese port authorities only work from 0700 to 1400 daily, so that a vessel arriving or wanting clearance outside those hours is hamstrung—however 'welcome to Lebanon' she may be.

It was a struggle to leave Tripoli, for the Customs officers had pounced on a more important customer than us in the shape of a big freighter and we had to wait an hour or two before we could get clearance, planned for 0700. We discovered that there was now only one approach buoy outside the harbour, instead of the two shown on the Admiralty chart. Authorities in these parts seem terribly slow in telling other people what they are up to.

The coastwise passage northwards towards the Syrian border was made in perfect weather. The water here is pretty shallow, usually an average of about 5 fathoms, so this has something to do with it. We took the inshore channel up inside the shoals of Mak Rud and finally anchored in the southerly cove of Rouad Island (called Arvad by the Lebanese) about midday. The approach was difficult, for a considerable amount of new construction was in progress, designed, I am glad to say, to make the island's ports more secure. The works were not very well marked, but as the sun was so bright and the water so shallow, we were able to see the submerged works and a safe entry ensued. Rouad has two coves on its eastern side: I recommend the southerly, which we used.

No sooner had I dropped my hook than a boat set out from the shore carrying what I supposed to be officials alerted by my 'Q' flag. Instead of greeting me in the usual way, however, they left us open-mouthed by rushing forward and tearing down my Syrian courtesy flag. I simply did not know what on earth to do.

They then left without a word, rowed ashore and came back with another much larger and very similar flag. 'That,' they said, 'will cost you ten dollars!' The Phoenicians had obviously been here, too. Aghast at this display of greed, I protested that the flag I had been flying was quite big enough for us. (Captain Watts always sends me the right size and, to date, the right design, too!) However, after a great deal of shouting and gesticulating, they made me understand that the flag I had been flying was out of date since February 1958, when the latest revolution had caused a new design to be approved. True, the new and the old were very similar, but I naturally had to give way to local feelings, though in the end I did settle for a size smaller—final agreed price: one dollar. (Everyone talks in American dollars in these parts; sterling is out of date.)

Up went the one-dollar flag and everyone seemed pleased. Yet another boat appeared alongside, this time absolutely loaded to the gunwale with officials. Fortunately, one of them, a young fellow who said he had appeared on television in English at Beirut (where they all seem to want to go to work), was able to do a good job of translation. In the course of my yachting, I have had to speak, French, German, Italian, the Scandinavian languages, Greek and a little Turkish—but Arabic was really beyond me.

'Can we enter Syria here?'
'Yes.'
'No.'
'I don't know: I will telephone to Tartous opposite to ask.'
'Can we enter at Tartous?'
'Of course.'
'Certainly not.'
'We don't know.'

I gave them whisky, though I believe their religion rather discourages this. Confusion grew. I abandoned them and went below to lunch. An hour later the message came from the shore.

'You cannot enter Syria here.'

'You cannot enter it at Tartous either.'

'You must clear at Lattakia [40 miles north] and then you can go where you like.'

This was all displeasing and I made myself clear on this point. We had come to visit the superb Crusader Castle of Krak des Chevaliers, which lay directly inland from Tartous and to have to go 40 miles north to Lattakia and then back again seemed absurd. But my interpreter was adamant. 'Welcome to Syria,' he would throw in now and then, with a smile.

It did emerge, however, that Tartous, where a new port was nearing completion under the auspices of a Yugoslav concern (also responsible for the improvements at Rouad) would be declared open to shipping in winter 1965–6, after which date Syria would have two ports of entry, Lattakia in the north and Tartous in the south. Until then, it was Lattakia or nothing, though a vague hint was dropped that possibly Banyas, a half-way house between them, would do. Meanwhile, did we want to go ashore for a while at Rouad? Price for use of boat—one Syrian pound—maybe two, it would depend. Did we want to take photographs? Yes? Perhaps it could be arranged?

Amusing though this approach to the tourist certainly was, we got a bit fed up with it after a while. Long faces were pulled when I told them that I did not want to go ashore, that I would take no photographs and that I was sailing forthwith. A night at Rouad would perhaps have been nice, especially as the southern harbour has now been made very much safer and the holding looked good, but an atmosphere of mutual trust and dependability still remained to be established.

So we sailed for Banyas. It was a beautiful and interesting trip in shoal waters. Our course took us within half a cable of the seaward end of the huge new breakwater the Yugoslavs have built to contain the outer port of Tartous, which now encloses the former smaller port of El Mina, which I suppose will continue as a boat harbour. Thence coastwise past Ipsiri islet and for some time in shoal waters past Markab Castle perched on an eminence overlooking the shore, until finally the oil storage tanks of the Irak Petroleum Company at Banyas came into view and we set course for the Banyas boat harbour, making fast there in ideal surroundings soon after tea. It had been an amusing and pleasant trip.

The Syrians who received us at Banyas were very helpful. They had never had to deal with a yacht before and we were an object of some curiosity. Fortunately, the harbour master spoke French. I explained to him that we wanted to go to Krak des Chevaliers and he said he would telephone to Lattakia and try to get us permission to enter his country at Banyas, thus saving us a lot of trouble. After the formalities were over and we had dined, I went up to the compound of the Irak Petroleum Company and tried to make a call on the management, but found no one around. The clocks had been put forward an hour (Syrian time) and we were already fairly late.

Next morning we watered and washed down and we had a call from the company's Terminal Superintendent, Captain Gross, who was, I hoped, as glad to see us as we were to see him. New faces must be at a premium in this part of the world. He most kindly arranged for us to be able to fuel (nothing duty-free here), made arrangements for a taxi to Krak des Chevaliers and invited us up to a film show in the mess that evening. In such a delightful port, we should have guessed that it was too good to last.

The blow fell at lunch-time. Captain Gross reappeared with the news that the manager, Mr Banister, disapproved of our presence and that we must leave. In ancient times he would have been beheaded for bringing such bad tidings, but as it was, we took the news with calm and dignity. I never believe in staying where you are not wanted, so we let go at once, hurriedly cancelling our arrangements for laundry which we had just carefully made and leaving behind our outboard motor which the company's mechanics were in process of repairing.

I suppose this is the first time that a British yacht flying the Blue Ensign of Her Majesty's Fleet has been turned out of a port, and by order of a British subject at that. However, we bore no ill-will, applying ourselves rather to trying to determine what had caused our banishment. I had heard from the Syrians that this port was privately owned by the Irak Petroleum Company, who would not even allow Syrian vessels to use it. It was strictly reserved for the company's craft. Maybe this was the reason for our presence causing embarrassment. It would have been nice to know. Neither the Admiralty Pilot Book, nor the Admiralty chart makes any mention of this being a 'private' port, nor does Henry Denham in his guidebook mention this angle, confining himself to the remark that it is 'well sheltered'. I suppose if someone builds a private port they can do what they like with it: but I do feel strongly that ports of this kind should be clearly indicated as such. 'Welcome to Syria.'

I was thus faced with the alternative of retracing my steps a mile or two south and making the anchorage of Banyas town—where in the prevailing weather I think we would have passed a quiet night—or of continuing northward to Lattakia, some 3 hours for me. I was expecting mail at Lattakia, so I decided to push on north, threading my way through the oil terminals and loading buoys that lie in some numbers off this coast.

When I arrived inside Lattakia pierheads about 6 o'clock I was sorry I had not gone back to Banyas town. Lattakia appeared quite unsuitable for a yacht. The wind at that moment was northerly, with a resultant swell all over the harbour. The outer port was full of shipping of many nationalities, and the inner port, for which we made cautiously, was full of swell and barges. The only protected berth was occupied by some Syrian warships and I was sure we would not be allowed to join them. I was greatly relieved in my uncertainties when we were hailed from the light tower to port on entering the inner harbour by a pilot and directed to go alongside the quay astern of the warships. But on arrival, there was not enough room to fit in, so I was compelled to go stern to the quay and risk being squashed by a gaggle of barges alongside me. However, we were glad to be fast at last and looked forward to going ashore. Imagine our disappointment when the pilot on duty (a good type) came around and told us that in Syrian ports the working hours ended at 1400, after which it was impossible to obtain clearance. 'Welcome to Syria,' he added.

So there we were, in a dirty commercial berth, unable to go ashore. We played bridge far into the night, just to show them. Punctually at 0730 next morning we had a visit from the local authorities, who did not seem at all distressed by our having had to suffer from their idleness. They were correct, polite and efficient and we were given passes for going ashore. I went off to fix a taxi and was at once hailed by a fellow on a motor-bike who offered me a lift. I found it a little difficult to explain, while being bounced around Lattakia harbour at a rate of knots that all I wanted was to find a taxi who would take us for a drive. The man finally dumped me at a Bulgarian ship unloading chemicals and demanded money. I explained that I had not asked to be brought here, that I was not aware that he had the right to ask for money and that anyway, I had none. We were in the midst of each having a thrombosis when an English-speaking Customs man appeared and explained to me that this man was, in fact, a phenomenon peculiar to Syria—a 'motor-bike taxi' and he was quite entitled to receive a fare. I was about to explode when he made the classic remark 'Welcome to Syria', which fortunately broke the ice as far as I was concerned. How can one be angry in the face of such ingenuousness?

We did finally find a rather elderly taxi—driven by a man called 'Sergeant'—with the aid of a tourist bureau—and for the agreed price of £11 sterling we set off for Krak des Chevaliers in a mood of resignation tinged with despair. We picked up our outboard motor at the IPC, drove straight through Banyas town, which appeared very uninviting, and made the steep ascent to Markab Castle, one of a chain of Crusader castles dominating this coast, whence the superb view and intelligent guide began to put us back in good humour. On arrival at Tartous, where there is a twelfth-century cathedral turned museum (and extremely well arranged) our car broke down: evidently the thought of a further 50 miles to Krak was too much for it. Sergeant brought us the news during lunch and there was a hint of 'more money', the bane of travellers in the Levant, being charged. Finally another car was procured and the journey completed (a never-to-be-forgotten experience). For some 20 miles on the return journey we were treated to a terrifying argument between the sub-leased driver and our 'Sergeant' on who was going to pay how much money to whom. By preserving a discreet silence we managed to keep out of the argument and triumphantly paid our 'Sergeant' exactly what we said we would—plus tip. This must be the first time in local tourism that this had ever happened. We had pioneered for culture.

The town of Lattakia is hardly conducive to gaiety; we dined quietly aboard. After dinner, the pilots helped me to go shopping for things like bread, ice and vegetables, all readily available. There was a considerable argument with the taximan—needless to say—and every port official seemed anxious to extract cigarettes and money from me. The harbour master promised to clear us early next morning—we had a long way to go.

At the appointed hour next day no one was in sight except the faithful 'Sergeant', come to see us off. The harbour master was nowhere to be seen, though the police and Customs papers were all in order to go. 'Sergeant' went off in search and came back empty-handed. There was really nothing to do except say we were sailing, so I slipped and began to move towards the pierheads. No good. A furious-looking launch came chasing after us, the harbour master, resplendent in whites, at the prow. 'Stop! You have not paid your harbour dues!'

'How much?'

Endless calculations began, nobody agreeing.

'How much did you pay in Rouad?'

'A dollar,' I guessed.

'O.K. Give me a dollar.'

We were liberated. 'Welcome to Syria.'

I do hope what I have written on yachting in Syria and the Lebanon will not be misunderstood. No one could possibly say that either country is yet attuned to this form of *grand tourisme*, though the time might well come when things will move forward in this direction. A timid soul should certainly not attempt the experience; for it can be depressing and unnerving. But to the old motor-boat salt such as myself countries like this represent a challenge. And only by going there—and showing them that one is really a tourist and not a smuggler or a spy—can the atmosphere eventually be created when they will get used to us going there in large numbers—with the financial advantages it must bring them. Neither the Syrian nor the Lebanese coastline is exceptionally beautiful and the harbours are few, but the countries themselves are absorbingly interesting, the inland excursions many and superb and—once you know how to deal with the people much better than I do—they might well take a yachtsman to their heart. 'Welcome to Lebanon'—'Welcome to Syria.' Maybe one day they will really mean it. Maybe they do now—in a way.

With Lattakia and its memories of Syria just a smudge on the horizon, I had to face 11 hours of solid plugging before making my first Turkish port of entry at Iskenderun, formerly known as Alexandretta. The swell was south-westerly, which put it on my port quarter, sufficiently uncomfortable for me to wonder whether, after all, it might not be nice to put into Bassite Bay, a 'resort' type of anchorage where the Syrians had told me one would be allowed to land, despite having cleared for 'foreign'. Bassite is just on the Syrian side of the Turkish border and is the only anchorage sheltered from the prevailing summer sou'-westerlies hereabouts, with the exception of El Mina, which is well protected by a mole, but which is prohibited to civilian craft.

I decided to push on. The prospect of arriving in Turkey before nightfall and relaxing for a couple of days ashore was attractive. Soon after lunch, and in perfect weather, I reckoned we were off the ancient port of Seleucia, once the seaport of Roman Antioch, greatest city of the world. The guide-books said it was now silted up, but that the River Orontes, which still flowed into the sea close by, could just possibly be entered across its bar in certain weathers, and the passage up to Antioch sounded attractive on paper. I always enjoy exploring these difficult possibilities. But the prospect of going aground in the mouth of a fast-flowing river reminded me too much of an experience I once had in the estuary of the Seine when over-taken by the *mascaret*, or tidal bore. Once was enough; on we went.

After the first 50 miles, we made the impressive headland of Cape Resülhinzir, which comes sheer down into the sea and houses a welcoming lighthouse. The scenery here and indeed onwards to Iskenderun is very fine indeed. Yet another ruined Crusader castle, once belonging to the La Roche family and known as the Rock of Roissel, came into view. It was besieged in 1188 by Saladin, whose tomb I had visited the other day in Damascus. Time for lunch and I entered the attractive Bay of Arsuz, dropped the hook and had a meal and a swim. This place offers good pro-tection from all winds from west through south around to north-east and, if one were not in too great a hurry, would make a convenient stopping-place. It is not, however, a port of entry.

On approaching Iskenderun an hour or so later, I tried to call up the harbour radio station to announce our arrival. Like many other minor Turkish ports, it is listed in the Admiralty list of coastal stations as being manned continuously. Not a sound came in reply to my impassioned entreaties. I afterwards learned that this little station is, in fact, only manned when a vessel is expected and then only if her agent asks the port authorities for it to be opened.

Here we were at last. Ringed by friendly mountains, the Bay of Isken-derun offered a perfect night anchorage off the attractive town. At first we tried to enter the small artificial port marked on the chart, but when I saw how unsuitable it looked, being seriously encumbered with lighters, I put about and dropped my anchor among the shipping in the bay. This varied from minor warships through coastal passenger steamers to the usual caique type of coastal trader. The best berth was about 100 yards off the town pier, which offered reasonably good landing facilities, if a little crowded with ferries plying for hire. We put our clocks back an hour, having arrived in an area of Eastern European Standard Time, after Syrian Summer Time.

In Lattakia the harbour master had demanded to see our log, to make sure that we had not been to an Israeli port, and I wondered if the Turks would be interested in our log book, too. The Arab peoples consider themselves in a state of war with Israel and treat anyone having to do with that country as a potential enemy. When they arrived aboard us in a smart launch, however, the Turkish authorities were quite uninterested in such matters. They seemed only to want to know how best they could help us. Iskenderun provided one of the warmest welcomes I have ever had in the Mediterranean.

At first I was a little dismayed that an agent was in the welcoming party, as my experience of these people has not always been a happy one. But this agent quickly assured me that he wanted no fee for his services. Like so many in these parts, Michel Naccache, for so he was called, turned out to be a Christian Arab, one of the Maronite sect of Roman Catholics whose persuasion dates back to the time of the Crusades. He looked after us like a father all the while we were in his port, introducing us to his friends, taking us out to a superb dinner and generally seeing that we had all we wanted. We so much enjoyed our stay in Iskenderun, where the anchorage was mercifully quiet, that we prolonged our visit by a day. I actually managed to get one of my cameras mended: the shops were excellent. A snag was that, being at anchor, we could not get fresh water without a lot of trouble, but we had watered at Banyas and had enough for a while.

I hired a taxi (about £5 for the day) and motored across the spectacular pass known as the Gates of Syria, where the modern road winds up and down the mountain in a series of terrifying bends, carrying heavy traffic— as indeed it has done throughout the ages, from camels to motor-cars. It takes about 2 hours to get to Antioch, which we found disappointing, with the exception of some very fine mosaics in the museum and a curious grotto in some cliffs outside the town, known as St Peter's Grotto, where it is said the early Christians used to worship to avoid persecution. The famous

Orontes River was just a muddy stream: I was glad we had not tried to ascend it.

The drive seawards from Antioch to the ruins of the old port of Seleucia was, however, most rewarding, and the ruins themselves were of very great interest to anyone concerned with harbours. Remains of the moles, the canal leading inshore and the actual basin are still clearly visible—all high and dry, of course. Some of the Turkish Customs guards from the local guard house led me around the ancient rock channel, which was a major feat of engineering performed in the times of Vespasian and Titus (as indeed a plaque recalls) and served to divert a mountain torrent from the town. All around were extensive rock tombs which, if my guides had had their way, I would have been visiting for weeks.

That evening we gave a small party aboard for local officials and their families. I was always under the impression that Mohammedans, which most of them were, were forbidden by the Koran to drink alcohol: this impression has now been changed.

I was in two minds whether to push on westwards now towards Mersin and points west or to dally around in the Gulf of Iskenderun for another day, perhaps visiting the ancient Genoese port of Ayas, and maybe even ascending the Çeyhan River. I had heard that the estuary of this, the largest river in southern Turkey, was the haunt of pelicans, birds that have always intrigued me. Finally, I decided on going westwards: it was already September 26 and I did not want to risk staying so late in the season that bad weather might develop. Everything so far had been so very good. The 34 sea-miles from Iskenderun to the anchorage of Karataş, where I had decided to spend the night, were easily accomplished, though navigation along the coast was not all that easy, due to the very low shores. The discoloration of the sea due to the River Çeyhan's effluence was very marked. At Karataş, we anchored in a position 4 miles east-north-east of Cape Fener off a sandy beach. This was all right while the day breeze blew, but at night the wind changed and we had a very uncomfortable time. We should have taken the advice of the locals, who rowed out to tell us, and anchored inside the islands off the village. Nevertheless, we managed to get in some good dinghy sailing. The attractions ashore seemed very limited.

Karataş to Mersin was a pleasing coastal run, though again the shoreline provided nothing of interest. The harbour installations are visible at sea for many miles. I went at first to a basin on the western side of the port marked 'Yacht basin' on the chart, but this was obviously quite hopeless. There was a concentration of destroyers at anchor in the main harbour and I went alongside one of them, who directed us to the commercial quay, where, after several changes of berth, we were able to get fresh water at last and wash down.

Despite the attentions of Mr Naccache's firm of agents (once more free gratis and for nothing) we voted Mersin the most unattractive Turkish port we had ever visited. The harbour itself was without interest, and to get to the town one had to walk across quite a bit of depressing wasteland, only to find that there was nothing to see on arrival. But supplies of all kinds, including ice, were excellent.

In sharp contrast to the rather uninteresting coastline of the previous two days, all that followed was magnificent. Slipping from Mersin at 0600 to avoid yet another change of berth, we followed the coast closely in 4 or 5 fathoms of water, noting the increasingly beautiful contours and ancient monuments as we proceeded. First came Viranşehir (once the ancient port of Soli, now silted). Through the glasses, we could just make out the port and aqueduct. It was here that the expression 'solecism' was coined, the inhabitants of Soli through various occupations having forgotten the correct use of their native Greek tongue.

To test its value as a port of refuge, I put into the tiny artificial port of Lamas, 25 miles west of Mersin. There was a steamer buoy rusting away outside the port, but not a sign of life or indeed of any facility within. Nevertheless, it is nice to know it is there.

I have never seen anything like the coastline between Lamas and Kizkalezi, 8 miles farther on. There were ruins everywhere. To identify them would be quite impossible. We were all glued to the glasses through-out the morning, as aqueducts, theatres, temples and tombs followed each other in rapid succession. Does anyone know these things are there? Or what they are? Finally, the glory of the twin castles of Kizkalezi itself unfolded as we rounded a cape. I anchored in 2 fathoms, sand, inside the pier leading to the large castle and went ashore in the dinghy to ask where a convenient night anchorage might be found. A Turkish Customs guard obligingly offered to pilot us to a cove called Narlik, not mentioned by name on the chart, but lying 2 miles farther west. The presence of a 'motel' on the beach did not mar the splendour of the two castles, both built by Armenian kings, and originally connected by a sea wall, which has disappeared. The sea castle is still known as 'The Maiden's Castle'. Legend has it that one of the kings had a beautiful daughter about whom it was prophesied that she would die of the bite of a snake. Horrified at this prospect, the king had her shut up in the 'Sea Castle', where she languished, safe but bored, until one day someone introduced an adder in a basket of vegetables and she met her unhappy end. Neither castle merits an entry, as both are sadly decaying, but the sight of them from outside is breath-taking. It is a pity that the sea-breeze, which springs up punctually each day at midday, makes the anchorage untenable.

Did you know that cows drank sea-water? They do at Narlik. An ice-cold underground river runs out into the head of the cove over the bottom of fine sand and is much appreciated by thirsty cattle. Narlik is not an ideal anchorage, as it is exposed eastward, but it is the best locally and at least in day-time in summer is perfectly safe. I laid out an anchor and a long stern line ashore and, profiting from the kindness of some Turks who lent me their car, drove myself along the coast to admire its marvels more closely and up to a terrifying pair of chasms carved out of the mountains by the underground river and locally known as 'Heaven and Hell'. Bathing in Narlik Cove was a curious experience, with alternate layers of hot and cold water to choose from.

By now we had established a daily pattern of winds which I suppose may be taken to represent summer conditions along this fabulous coast. From 2100 to 1200 next day, the winds seemed invariably to blow lightly from south east, unless there was a calm, which often happened. Regular as clockwork at midday the wind would shift to north east or north west and blow light to moderate until the evening. One could plan one's day accordingly. It is as well to know of these things, for there are virtually no ports on this long stretch of coast and one has to depend on what natural anchorages one can find.

Gilindire, former terminal of a steamer service to Cyprus, and some 50 miles west of Narlik, was one of these and there I planned to spend the following night. The little place has sadly decayed since its terminal days, but the inhabitants were extremely kind. I was taken for a drive on a tractor to view some local farms. The town provides no fresh water, no ice and very few provisions. The stone pier is now collapsing. There is about 4 ft of water at its head and it is best to lie off in 2 fathoms and secure a stern line. The children here were particularly exasperating.

Between Gilindire and Alanya, the next safe night stop, is a long 80-mile run. It is essential to break it at Anamur Castle, which is a sight one dare not miss. We accordingly slipped from Gilindire at o600 and made Anamur Castle at o915, well before the onslaught of any winds, so that we were able to anchor and photograph it to our hearts' content. The castle, which lies on an exposed sandy beach, seems virtually intact. It has three wards and thirty-six towers, and like Kizkalezi, was built by the Armenian kings, being later occupied by Crusaders. I did not go ashore, being anxious to press on to Alanya. If you must land, however, I suggest spending the night off the quay at Anamur village, a few miles west, and getting some sort of transport to the castle in the early hours before the wind rises.

All that afternoon we plugged on towards Alanya. It was an absorbing trip, close inshore beneath the majestic cliffs of the lower Taurus range, along which a newly built road struggled to keep a foothold. Everywhere on the southern slopes were banana plantations. Day temperatures now had dropped to about 95° Fahrenheit in the shade. The wind was less trying than we had expected, calms and light south easterlies being the general rule, with the anticipated westerlies not showing up until late afternoon and then only moderately.

The best berth for a yacht at Alanya is stern to one of the lower excrescences on the wooden and concrete jetty there. There is heaps of water at this jetty and fresh water is laid on to the end of it. The ice factory, we learned, had unfortunately broken down, but we got an excellent meal in the town. The Norwegian cruise vessel *Meteor* was alongside when we berthed and sailed shortly afterwards. No less than eight gentlemen boarded us to perform the formalities, but when they saw that we had arrived from another Turkish port the business was quickly over. Of wind there was none and I looked forward to a quiet night beneath the battlements.

Henry Denham, in his book *The Eastern Mediterranean*, says that Alanya is one of the most imposing places on the Pamphilian coast. I agree with him. Up early next morning, I was glad to get enough light to photograph the fortress that overlooks the town, as well as the curious octagonal tower near the root of the quay. From seven o'clock until midday we enjoyed a perfect calm run along the coast as far as Side, which is also known, as so often happens in Turkey, as Eski Antalya or even Selimiye. Side was certainly the name by which it was known when it was built 3,000 years ago.

The coastal run remained extremely lovely, though less grandiose than the cliffs before Alanya. On arrival off Side, the light wind was still south east, so I chose to anchor in 2 fathoms, sand, inside the ancient mole to the north-west of the promontory, where we lay undisturbed. I dinghied ashore to call on some Turkish friends who kept a restaurant there, and to my surprise they took me to have a drink with some delightful American journalists who had recently come to live there. During my stay I met quite a lot of foreigners, who have formed a sort of colony in this delightful place, as yet unspoiled by excessive 'tourism'. The village has sprung up among the ruins of the ancient city, so that it is quite normal to find oneself sitting on a column of the Temple of Athena, or even making fast one's dinghy to a marble bollard from the base of a Roman sarcophagus.

The uncrowned king of Side is Sakir Kabaagac, who keeps a hotel-restaurant where he entertains on a lavish scale, speaks four foreign languages and has travelled all over the world. Among the sights that he and his family showed me was quite the best museum that I have seen in Turkey, the magnificent theatre of Side, built to hold 15,000 people and the site of the Temple of Athena, in whose honour games used to be held here. Side at evening-time has a curious other-world feeling as the sun sets over the ruins and leaves the place to its memories. I was distressed to find, on making *September Tide* after a good dinner, that the wind had changed to north-west and we were rolling around in our anchorage. We should really have shifted berth to the south-eastern anchorage, but I was too lazy. However, the wind dropped during the night and with it the swell. We had some ice (rather expensive at £T5 a bar) sent down from Manavgat, the local town.

The coast between Side and Antalya is not very interesting, except near Antalya itself, when it forms cliffs again and there is a curious waterfall descending straight into the sea. The little port of Antalya is so small and hidden that one does not see the entry until almost on top of it. Larger vessels have to anchor off. Spurning the services of a pilot boat that came out to meet me, I steered straight for the harbour mouth, having entered which, I at once dropped the hook in the centre near some caiques at anchor and edged my stern in towards the western side of the harbour. After considerable manoeuvring in rather nebulous depths of water, we managed to make fast a couple of stern lines and get a gangway near the shore on the topping lift. It was not a very happy arrangement, but at least it was better than having to use the dinghy each time we went ashore. The port, though possessing plenty of charm, leaves much to be desired from a practical point of view. There are rocks everywhere, the only practical berth is almost always occupied (at the head of the harbour), large caiques encumber the centre, and the water which is alleged to be laid on at the quay is, in fact, some distance away behind some houses and could, I was told, only be used by permission of the Customs. Indeed, the Customs, although they gave me no trouble, are a perfect nuisance at this little place. I invited some Turks for drinks aboard and it was a very long time before the Customs would let them come. It is surprising to me how people will tolerate this sort of thing in their own country. Imagine it happening in Poole or on the Hamble!

Restrictions did not, apparently, apply to the activities of the local agent, who was quick on the scene with ice and stores. I made the mistake of not insisting on a service fee being agreed in advance, so that later on I had a set-to about what we were to pay for his unsolicited efforts. This was, I fear, rather the atmosphere in this tourist-conscious little town, where on more than one occasion I found myself unwittingly paying enormous prices for very little in return. I suppose one has to suffer these things as a defenceless foreigner in tourist places. I would have done better to go at once to Madame Nermin, who keeps the local tourist shop, and thrust myself on to her mercies. Through her, I met a number of delightful Turks, who entertained us royally during our stay.

One of the tourist 'musts' at Antalya is a visit to Aspendos, where there is a strange vast barn of a Roman theatre looking like an unfinished block of modern flats. I also made a trip to Perga, which has 3,000 years' worth of assorted and entertaining ruins to offer. The modern town of Antalya is entirely without interest, but the old houses surrounding the port are enchanting. I trust they will be well preserved and not fall victims to the current Turkish vogue of only wanting the 'modern' to survive.

Antalya is well worth a visit and is a good centre for communications, being connected to the Turkish airways system. Its port is unsuited to most yachts, but I was glad to hear that a new harbour, on a much larger scale, is to be built to the west of the town, where beach meets cliffs, and is expected to be opened in 1970.

It was already October 5 when we finally said good-bye to our Turkish friends—who came to see us off—at Antalya and set course southwards towards Cape Gelidonya and the eastern approaches to the Aegean. The coastline here is the wildest and most majestic in all Turkey. There are no ports, few anchorages and no people. The mountains are often capped with snow and the whole region resembles the French Riviera as I suppose it was before it was ever 'discovered'.

I had been advised to have a look at the ruins of ancient Phaselis, where there were two anchorages and a diminutive ancient port in which the chart showed 1 fathom—enough for me—both inside and in the entry. Edging my way carefully towards it, I soon saw the moles, now awash. There was a slight following sea, engendered by the south-east wind. As my bows entered the old pierheads, I knew with a sudden feeling of despair that we were aground. No amount of going hard astern both motors moved me. A launch appeared around a distant cape and I fired a distress rocket, to which she paid no attention. The sea was rising, each wave throwing me farther on to the rocks—there was not a soul for miles. Then the miracle happened—perhaps the increasing waves helped—and we moved slowly astern to safety. The Admiralty chart was obviously inadequate, if not misleading, for there was, in fact, only about 4 ft of water in the harbour mouth. Chastened by this sad experience, I decided to abandon any thought of even anchoring off Phaselis, whose ruins were by now clearly visible, and we altered course southwards again to what we knew to be a safe anchorage at Porto Cinoviz (Porto Genovese) just north of Cape Gelidonya. Here, in surroundings of idyllic quiet and beauty, we anchored and put a stern line ashore, the boat's nose pointing to the Taurus.

I was greatly tempted to emulate my predecessor Goeran Schildt and pay a visit to the fabled Chimaera 'volcano' in the Bay of Cirali, only a mile or two distant. I had learned in Antalya, however, that to get to the volcano involved anchoring offshore and walking some 2 miles through scrub in each direction to find this curious little flame of sulphurous gas. I finally decided to abandon the idea and instead to pass seawards of the island of Sulu, there to admire the fine natural arch. Thence our much-altered course took us close in to Cape Gelidonya—like Cape Malea at the south end of the Peloponnese, an object of great fear to the ancients—on which cape there is the unusual phenomenon of two lighthouses, one to help offshore navigation and the other, weaker, to prevent one hitting the seaward extremity of the cape itself. In perfect weather, we anchored for lunch at Yali, or Goekkaya, cove, continuing later to our favourite spot off Kekova Castle for the night. This time the mosquitoes did not trouble us, for already it was past their season. The Lycian tombs were still there, leaning like tired sentinels down from their embattled hills: one was half submerged in the tranquil waters of the fjord.

And so to Kaş, to clear and say farewell to Turkey, at least for this season; and on to Castellorizzo, to say 'Yasu' once more to the Greeks, to fill up with fuel and to embark on the 70-mile trip to Rhodes again. I had been tempted to continue via my favourite anchorage at Yorgun Koeyu as far as Fethiye, but the sands of time were running out. As we sailed for Rhodes, the winds started to rise and by dawn, as we approached Rhodes town, a moderate northerly ruled the seas. We were truly entering the Aegean.

Rhodes had a new harbour master—a nice helpful fellow—and there was mail awaiting us. The Scandinavian tourists were fewer and a general atmosphere of *fin de saison* lay over the town. I planned a return trip to Vouliagmeni (Piraeus) to last me 6 days. Alas! we had not reckoned with the treacherous Aegean. We were weather-bound at Rhodes for 2 days— in good company, even John Bloom's *Ariane III* decided to postpone sailing. A day at Kos; a day at Leros, where the pathetic British cemetery of the dead of a Commando raid of the last war adorns the windswept coast and the bedraggled Italian-built barracks house now a vast and rather unkempt lunatic asylum; a day in Patmos, where there was a strange Swiss lady who claimed to have the same revelation as St John; a night in the newly equipped Mykonos anchorage of Ornos Bay; an appalling crossing to Tinos and 2 days in Gavrion on Andros Island before having our sails carried away crossing the Doro Channel to Euboea; whence south to Cape Sounion and home. The Aegean indeed lived up to its unpleasing reputation.

We had gone 1,502 nautical miles since we left Rhodes on this cruise 35 days ago, visited five countries, endless ports and anchorages, and seen all—well, almost all, of the places we had set out hearts upon to visit, and, except for the return journey in the Aegean, been smiled upon by Providence all the way. I would gladly do it again.

On Going Foreign

*Do's and Don't's for the Seaborne Tyro
with a list of places where to buy foreign charts*

A yachtsman has not lived up to his title until he has 'been foreign'. Unfortunately, many people think that to take a yacht abroad is a major difficulty. They imagine fierce Customs men 'rummaging' their way from stem to stern, the crew meanwhile held prisoner in the forecastle, or preparing lists of misdemeanours carrying giant fines. Bellicose policemen lurk behind every bollard. Cohorts of petty officials, armed with sheaves of unintelligible forms, perch like vultures on the pierheads, ready to attack the innocent mariner and tear him to shreds.

It is not at all like that. Of course, things are strange, but isn't that part of the fun? Generally speaking, a British yachtsman going foreign has fewer horrors to face than a foreign yachtsman visiting our shores. The Continentals exercise their control in a more leisurely, less apparent way than we do. But they know what goes on, just the same.

The journey, naturally, requires preparation. Obviously passports are needed, though in none of the countries close to these islands are visas necessary. In larger yachts, which are sometimes apt to be treated like merchantmen, it is not strictly necessary for all the crew to have passports; a list of the crew who have 'signed on' for the voyage can be made out on a special form issued by the Ministry of Transport and known as an A.3 Form. When this is shown to the foreign authorities they simply give each man named on it a permit to go ashore in the precincts of the port and do not bother about passports. These forms can be obtained from the shipping offices in all major British ports and from our consular representatives abroad. It is certainly not worth while for a small yacht to bother about this 'signing on' except when she proposes visiting rather unusual places. For instance, when I cruised to East Germany and Poland in 1959, I made sure, when I got to Hamburg, that we were all 'signed on' on an A.3, so that were we to disappear completely to the salt-mines there would at least be some official record of our having done so! When I visit the Black Sea, I shall take care to do the same thing.

The ship herself needs identification. If she possesses a Certificate of British Registry, and it is strongly recommended that she should, this will be ample evidence and is universally accepted. Countries which issue temporary documents to enable the yacht to minimize formalities while coasting in their waters (such as Greece, Italy and Yugoslavia) will accept this as a basic document. There have been instances of yachts being stolen or having writs attached to them. To carry your certificate of registry will show that yours is not one of them. I remember arriving at Paimpol, in Brittany, some seasons ago while there was a hue and cry on for a motor yacht like mine that had disappeared from the Channel Islands while under writ. It was not until our certificate of registry had been duly vetted that the French Customs became their normal pleasant selves.

If she has no certificate of registry, she may be tempted to sail from her U.K. base on the strength of possessing the Revenue Form 29(Sale) and 30(Sale), both of which ensure that she is immune from any British import duties on return. But the purpose of this document is not to act as a yacht's 'passport' and it is questionable whether it will always, or, indeed, ever, be acceptable to foreign authorities. I strongly recommend every yachtsman to secure a Certificate of British Registration and never to rely on any other papers. By law, in fact, every vessel of over 15 tons net should be registered if going foreign, a fact which is sometimes forgotten. An unregistered vessel abroad is, moreover, not entitled to the protection of her flag.

So the passports and the Certificates of British Registry are all a yacht requires in the way of papers when going foreign in western Europe. In France, on arrival at the first port, the 'green book' (passport for the yacht) must be obtained from the Customs. If she means to navigate inland waterways in France, Belgium, Germany or the Netherlands, she may be asked to go through the same drill as a car used to undergo. That is, she may be asked to deposit a bond at the port of entry, equivalent to her value. This can usually be arranged through a local bank, which will get into touch with the owner's bank at home and so produce the required guarantee. But a simpler way around all this is merely to get an international '*Carnet de Passages en Douane*' from the A.A. or R.A.C. before starting, just the same as with a car.

It is never certain that these papers will be needed, but they sometimes are. Questions of this kind only arise if the yacht actually enters the country concerned; she can, for instance, go as far as Rouen up the Seine, or well into Belgium, Holland and through the Kiel Canal without technically 'entering' the countries concerned at all. In point of fact, the French never ask for a deposit for yachts going up to Paris and down again, and on two occasions I have even crossed the whole of France by canal without this question being raised. But on other occasions I have had to produce my papers, so it is as well to be prepared.

Money matters are much less of a problem than they used to be.

It sometimes happens that repairs are needed while abroad. Have no fear. Shipyards abound and the Continental mechanic usually does a first-class job and is often far more '*débrouillard*' than his British counterpart; which means that he can make bricks with very little straw. Be sure, however, to agree on the charges first, as far as possible.

Charts are important. The Admiralty charts, which are available in almost every major port, are, in my opinion, far better than the various 'yachting charts' now being produced. But neither the Admiralty charts nor those privately produced will show the necessary detail of all the complicated inshore passages in foreign countries. I found it quite impossible, for instance, to navigate in the 'Riddle of the Sands' areas inside the Friesians on Admiralty charts. The Dutch and German charts, which can be bought in almost every port along that coast, are an absolute *sine qua non*. The same applied when I navigated the west coast of Sweden. Only the local Swedish charts are really complete. In Danish waters it is a moot point whether our own Admiralty charts are sufficient: personally, I think they are. In Norway, however, I would not care to navigate the inner leads unless I had the Norwegian local charts.

The chance of running on a wartime mine is now remote for a yacht. The cautious will nevertheless like to arm themselves with the Admiralty's routeing instructions to merchant ships (short title: NEMEDRI) which can be obtained from most shipping offices. They show the swept channels clearly, especially for the Friesian and Danish waters. The NEMEDRI chartlets and instructions can be of considerable value in that they often indicate sea-marks not shown on the normal charts.

In addition to charts of the seaways, there are excellent maps produced (mostly in Paris) which show the course of the principal French rivers. I have used these for the Seine, the Marne, the Yonne and the Saône. For the Rhône, a pilot is essential and a map, except for one's own interest, is not needed. Some of the Belgian rivers have been treated in this way and I can recommend the maps, too. For the Rhine, the best publication is Swiss, though rather difficult to get hold of. There are various maps of the Dutch waterways, none of them quite satisfactory: use Admiralty charts where possible.

When navigating the French inland waterways, especially the great canal network, the only reliable publications are those officially compiled by the French Government. These consist of detailed maps and accompanying guide-books.

Duty-free stores are more readily available 'foreign' than in Britain to a small yacht. There is none of the irritating application of the 'Over 40 tons' rule; size of the vessel plays no part. Duty-free stores are available to a visitor at almost every major French port, and there is no attempt to prohibit their consumption in harbour (except possibly on the Riviera, where there has been a certain amount of cheating). In Belgian ports, one is almost forced to buy something! The Dutch tend to approximate their British colleagues and are more severe in their application of the rules, while the Germans are very easy-going. The Scandinavians have had a lot of trouble with smugglers and do not issue duty-free stores to yachts below 40 tons net, as in Britain. Scandinavian yachts thus make frequent visits to Kiel for stocking up and the Danish and Swedish Customs are unfortunately thus kept rather too much on the *qui vive*. The result is that they like to know just how much a foreigner is carrying, although, even after sealing, they are very reasonable about issuing it whenever called upon. In the Mediterranean, conditions are very lax. But do not be misled into thinking the local people don't know what is going on.

Do not forget the courtesy flags of the countries the yacht is going to visit.

Where a burgee is worn at the masthead, it is correct to wear the courtesy flag at the starboard yard. A hoist of the yacht's distinguishing letters looks nice on entering harbour, but is by no means essential. Pay great attention to flags and see that 'colours' and 'sunset' are done at the right time. The yacht is an ambassador. And don't forget to take a 'Q' flag and fly it until the yacht has been given 'pratique'; in some French ports they ask for it to be hauled down as soon as they come aboard, generally because they are too lazy to give proper clearance. But it is in every yachtsman's interest to fly it until after the formalities are over. A drink and a cigarette in the saloon are, by the way, much appreciated by the foreign officials, many of whom lead dreary lives. One can do much good this way.

I had almost forgotten the Admiralty Pilot Books, obtainable from all nautical bookstores. Though written for larger ships, much of the information they contain applies equally to yachts and none should venture far without them. One more point; if a visit is made to a foreign yacht club—especially the more distant ones—there is nothing they like more than to receive a burgee of the visiting yacht's club. Maybe they will give one of theirs in return. So take a few burgees—if they are a wee bit tattered, so much the better. *'Bon Voyage!'*

FOREIGN CHARTS AND PLANS

In almost all the areas covered in this volume, the British charts are perfectly adequate and indeed much the most reliable. Yugoslavia and its greatly complicated coastline is, of course, a notable exception. The following notes may be of value in the individual countries concerned. Remember that it is always much cheaper to buy our own charts at home rather than abroad, where import duties sometimes double their price.

Italy

The ordinary British Admiralty charts cover the whole Italian coastline in great and adequate detail and I cannot see any reason why use should be made of Italian publications. An exception is the area in the lagoons of Venice, which is not covered by British charts. For this, Italian charts should be bought locally. This is not always easy; try Compagnia Radio Maritima, Campo Santa Maria del Giglio, Venice.

Malta

When I wintered there in 1962-3, there was an excellent British Admiralty chart depot in Valletta, but I hear this has since packed up. However, it should be easy to buy any charts one wants at local shipchandlers.

Greece

The Greek Navy do issue their own

charts, but as these are all written in Greek characters, the average foreigner has difficulty in understanding them. There is a British Admiralty chart depot, rather expensive, in Piraeus, where (expensive) corrections can also be made rather slowly. British charts are extensively used by Greek vessels, which seem to me to be a guarantee of their reliability. In my experience, British charts for Greek waters are all that are required. Chart Agent: John S. Lazopoulos, 7 Astingos Street, Piraeus.

Turkey

As far as I have been able to discover, there are no Turkish charts. The British charts are quite adequate, except perhaps for some of the very small places along the south coast of Turkey, where as far as I could discover no surveys had been made since Captain Beaufort of wind-scale fame made his reconnnaissance there in the early nineteenth century. Chart Agent: The Sea Ship Supply Co. Ltd., Tophana Iskelesi Cad., 117, Istanbul.

Syria

Fortunately, the short Syrian coastline does not present any great problems and the British charts are perfectly adequate. Remember that Banyas boat harbour is private property (not stated on charts) and that Tartous port has now been opened to shipping.

Lebanon

British and French charts are mostly used in this area. I found that British charts were all that we required.

Cyprus

British Admiralty charts are available in Famagusta and the island waters have been very extensively and accurately surveyed.

Yugoslavia

British charts are suitable for all passages and offshore waters. They are inadequate for all the inner leads where yachts are likely to sail and here Yugoslav charts should be obtained. Unfortunately, these can normally be bought only from the Yugoslav chart depot at Split. This is located in the Harbour Master's building.

From a Traveller's Scrapbook

In case it may be of practical help, I have made this list of people and things in places I have visited. It is possible that a small percentage (though not much) may have been overtaken by the march of time, in which case I crave forgiveness.

Italy

ANZIO

Ship Chandler (can also arrange fuel):
Messrs Vechiarelli and Co. At quayside.

Shell Fuel Depot:
Giovanni Ponteggi, Via Nazzario
Sauro, 13. Tel.: 28016.

CIVITAVECCHIA

Ship Chandler (also arranges fuel):
Joseph Caruso and Son,
Piazza Vittorio Emmanuele, 32.
Tel.: 3147 or 3265.

CROTONE

Ship Chandler:
Filli Tricoli fu Giovanni, s.r.l.,
P.O. Box 2157.
Tel.: 21082 or 21127.

Fresh Water:
Laid on to the quay. It is usual to give

Lit. 1,000 for a fill, though I suspect this is well above the correct rate.

Fuel:
Available duty-free at the approximate price of Lit. 23 per litre for diesel. There is a Shell depot here.

ISCHIA

Shipyards:
S.p.a. 'Argita', Via Porto, 54.
Tel.: 52.
Signor Belletieri is the manager.

MESSINA

British Vice-Consul:
Home Tel.: 14370.
Office Tel.: 10135.

Ship Chandlers:
Giovanni Costa.
Giovanni Gallo. Tel.: 18405.

Fresh water: Laid on to the quays. Official

price is Lit. 90 per ton if arranged through harbour master. If not so arranged, extortionate demands are inevitable.

Fuel: Available duty-free.

Meteorological Service: Tel.: 11217.

NAPLES

Ship Chandlers (also arrange fuel):
Messrs R. Luise and Company,
Calata Porta Massa.
Tel.: 321176 and 329521.
Messrs J. Luise and Sons Ltd,
10 Via Marittima.
Tel.: 328085.

(The relationship between these two firms is not clear: they are reputedly the same family, but appear to be in competition.)

Ship Repairers and Engineers:
Umberto Carrino,
Molo Carmine, 31.
Tel.: 350842 and 301586.
Alfonso Apicella,
Via de Pretis, 19.
Tel.: 322004.

BRINDISI
Fuel:
Signor Pennetta.
Tel.: 21509.

Weather Forecasts:
The local airport (Tel.: 21419) has information.

VENICE
British Consulate:
Residence and Offices near the Academia Bridge on the Grand Canal. Very helpful to visiting yachts.

Ship Chandlers (also for duty-free stores):
Messrs Ligabue S.p.A.,

Piazzale Roma, 499.
Tel.: 85100.

Shipping Agent (large yachts only):
Agenzia Radonicich, Calle Vallaresso (near Harry's Bar).
Tel.: 85341.

Yacht Club and Good Berth:
Diporto Velico Veneziano, Sant' Elena.
Tel.: 31927.

Shipyards:
Cantiere Renato Novo, Serenella, Murano.
Tel.: 39792.
Cantiere 'Oscar' di Constantino Oscar e Cia,
Cannaregio, 815, Venice-San Giobbe.
Tel.: 29886.

Electricians and Plumbers:
Ditta Francisco Vignola,
Castello 1626, Sant' Elena.
Tel.: 23395.

Charts:
Compagnia Radio Maritima,
Campo Santa Maria del Giglio.

Fuel:
The companies can arrange this, but it is a very long and laborious process and should be avoided if possible.

Harbour Dues:
These seem to have been abolished for yachts in recent years.

Customs Documents:
A yacht arriving in Italy for a coastal cruise must acquire at her first port of call a transit document known as 'Costituto in Arrivo per il Naviglio da Diporto'. A small fee is charged. This document is shown on arrival at each port, where it is surrendered to the harbour office and fetched by the captain again on sailing.

Penalties are sometimes exacted if this is forgotten. This excellent system avoids the necessity for clearing Customs again at each port. It was originally introduced to limit the activities of smugglers, since greatly reduced.

Fuel:

The duty-free price is usually upwards of 1s. 2d. per gallon. Delivery charges are often sufficiently high to prevent it being worth while taking on fuel in quantities of less than about 200 gallons.

Fresh Water:

Prices and availability vary considerably from port to port. The price asked is usually far in excess of that officially authorized.

Bonded Stores:

Are available at the larger ports, such as Genoa, Naples, Civitavecchia and Bari. Spirits are generally available in reasonable split quantities, but the minimum deliverable quantity of cigarettes is 10,000. Things like fruit juices, tonic water and Coca-Cola are sometimes worth buying under bond.

Malta

Queen's Harbour Master:
Commander N. M. Mules, R.N.,
H.M. Naval Base, Malta.
Tel.: 877241.

Civil Harbour Master:
Captain Tabone,
Customs House Quay, Valletta.

Yacht Club:
Royal Malta Yacht Club,
Marsamxett Harbour.

Agencies:
Messrs Ripard, Larvan and Ripard Ltd,
P.O. Box 75, Malta.

Tel.: 31563.
Messrs F. E. Sullivan and Co. Ltd,
17 Barreira Wharf, Valletta.
Tel.: 22016.

Malta Government Tourist Office:
St John's Square, Valletta.
Tel.: 24444.
Information Officer:
Mr J. Muscat Drago.

Yard Work (of all kinds, including slipping):
Messrs Malta Drydocks,
Manoel Island Slipways, Malta.
Tel.: 22451.
Manager: Mr S. Kilgour.
Ass. Manager: Mr R. Riggs.
Foreman: Mr S. Sapiano.

Bonded Stores:
Messrs Saccone and Speed Ltd,
20 South Street, Valletta.
Tel.: 25275.

Ta Xbiex Marina. Tel.: 30695. Captain A. Podesta is the Harbour Master to the Marina. He is also Executive Secretary to the Yachting Centre Advisory Committee to Government.

Yugoslavia

Ports of Entry:
Bar, Zelenika, Dubrovnik, Korcula, Split, Sibenic, Mali Losinj, Rijeka, Pula and Koper.

Visas:
Are required, but, unless issued beforehand, are very easily obtained on the spot by British yachtsmen. They are issued for up to 30 days for 'crew' and up to 7 days for 'passengers'. The fee is $2 for crewmen and Din. 300 per passenger. Renewal is not difficult and can be done at the larger towns.

Money:

Rates at the time of going to press are about 3,500 dinar to the £ against traveller's cheques, but if dinar notes are sold in the sterling area the selling rate is 5,000 to the £. Yugoslav regulations permit the import of up to Din. 10,000 in notes and the export of up to Din. 5,000. As from January 1966 the dinar has had a couple of zeros knocked off it (on the French model) and is thus officially quoted at Din. 35 to the £.

Ship's Papers:

It is as well to carry the vessel's Certificate of Registry and to have Articles for the crew. A list of crew and passengers is required at every port—so it is wise to have a stock of these in readiness. On arrival at her port of entry, a yacht is given a 'transit log' on the Greek model which indicates at which places she may *not* call. These include the immediate vicinity of Brioni Island, the Islands of Hvis and Hvisevo and an area on the southern side of Kotor Fjord. I have also heard that yachts have had trouble at:

(i) Goli Island in the Gulf of Kvarner,
(ii) San Giovanni Island in the Lastovo group,
(iii) both ends of Mljet Island,
(iv) Glavat and adjacent islands,
(v) the western end of Solta Island,
(vi) one or two anchorages inside Hvar Island,
(vii) a wooded island at the approach to Rogoznica Bay,

so I do not imagine that the 'transit log' can be relied on for total protection. But the Yugoslav officials who ask you to move on generally do so quite politely, so, if in doubt, one must simply proceed on the basis of trial and error.

Customs:

They are usually courteous and give no trouble. They ask on arrival for a list of things like typewriters, binoculars, firearms, etc.

Harbour Dues:

Are now collected in the major ports, but are not excessive.

Fresh Water:

Good clean water is available at all the larger ports at reasonable rates. In the islands, it is in very short supply and should only be requested if really necessary.

Fuel:

Diesel fuel can be absurdly expensive. Avoid at all costs buying it through the State-owned agency 'Brodokomerc', who have to charge 16 U.S. cents a kilogram, which gives a sterling rate of about 5s. 0d. a gallon. If the harbour master will send a road tanker or allow the vessel to lie alongside the local fuel installation, it can be bought for half this price. I have fuelled in this way with success at Split, Dubrovnik and Pula.

Duty-free Stores:

The Yugoslav arrangements are excellent. The Brodokomerc stores have their H.Q. at Rijeka, but also have important branches at Dubrovnik, Split and Koper. At other ports, by giving 24 hours' notice, duty-free stores can be delivered from one of these places. All the usual duty-free stores can thus be easily obtained, with the unfortunate exception of fuel.

Weather Forecasts:

Difficult to obtain, with the exception of Split, where a meteorological centre exists and where the harbour office will obtain a forecast for a yacht.

Charts:

Unbelievably, these are only obtainable at Split, where the main depot exists. Fortunately, British charts need little implementation from Yugoslav sources.

Repairs:

Absolutely first-class and very reasonably priced. In my experience, this is the only country where, after working all day on a complicated electronic job, the men refused to take any payment, as they felt the fault had not been properly adjusted. Woodwork, especially, is of top quality. Spares are difficult.

Photography:

It is forbidden to photograph naval or military installations. This includes ships and—of course—sailors, soldiers, etc. Even policemen must not be photographed.

Fishing:

Line fishing is free. Underwater fishing with air bottles is prohibited. Skin diving without air bottles is allowed against absurdly high payments (about 15s. per head per day) and then only in the immediate vicinity of the office that issued the permit. This means that skin diving is virtually impossible from a cruising yacht.

Navigation Marks:

Excellent.

Weather:

The notorious 'Bora' (a north to northeast wind) is the only real trouble and then only in winter. It almost never appears in July and August and only very rarely in other non-winter months. No fogs, though occasional morning mists. The Sirocco (a south to south-east wind) is apt to appear occasionally from October onwards throughout the winter. Telephone for forecasts: Split 2751.

Language:

Italian seems to be the lingua franca, though German is much spoken in the north. English and French are secondary. The only Serbo-Croat words we mastered were 'debre', meaning 'good', and 'Giveli', which you say when you have a drink. That seemed quite enough.

Gas Bottles:

May be filled, usually at about $1 a fill, plus transport costs, in the main centres.

Greece

Ports of Entry (where long-term clearance can be had):

Corfu Town, Preveza, Argostoli (Cephallonia), Patras, Kalamata, Piraeus, Vouliagmeni, Syros, Lavrion, Khalkis, Salonica, Kavalla, Alexandropoulis, Lemnos, Mytilene, Chios, Samos (Tigani), Kos, Rhodes, Iraklion and Kania (Crete) are the main ports of entry. A vessel entering Greece at a port not so classified should go at once to the nearest port of entry to secure her 'transit log'.

Customs Documents:

A yacht is issued with a 'transit log' on arrival at her first port of entry and this is her 'passport' as long as she is in Greek waters. It must be shown on demand and avoids the necessity of repeated Customs clearances at Greek ports during her stay.

Fuel and Fresh Water:

These are available on demand at all the eighty-eight 'Yacht Stations' established in Greek waters. The Yacht Stations are quayside installations offering fuel and fresh water in storage tanks at points marked by diagonal blue-and-yellow stripes and a blue flag. Fuel usually costs between 1s. 9d. and 2s. 3d. per gallon for diesel fuel and fresh water costs 5s. a ton.

Harbour and Sanitary Dues:
Harbour dues have been abolished for yachts making short visits, though some of the smaller ports occasionally levy them still. Sanitary dues are compulsory (with receipts) for yachts of over 21 tons net and have a considerable nuisance value.

Charts:
The British Admiralty charts for Greek waters are all that are required. They are available at Piraeus (see below). Their local price is about double the British figure, due to high import duties.

Duty-free Stores:
The usual line of duty-free stores, including cigarettes, cigars, spirits and wines, is available in Piraeus only.

Meteorological Forecasts:
In 1965 the Greek National Broadcasting system started to broadcast forecasts of the day's weather in English at approximately 0715 and 1950 daily. All Greek waters are covered and the wavelength is 412 metres. The Athens Shipping Radio Station issues a daily Mafor forecast on 2,590 kcs. at 1001 and 2215, with the numbers read in English. A forecast may also be obtained by telephoning the Athens Meteorological Station (see below). Athens radio is not a very good station, from a yacht's point of view, due largely to its faulty emplacement. A new station is to be built on the Peloponnese from which a great improvement is expected.

ATHENS-PIRAEUS-VOULIAGMENI
Yacht Brokers and Agents:
Messrs Costas Nicolaides and Costas Leggeris,
Hellas Yachting,
4 Kriezotou Street, Athens.
Tel.: 625698.

Messrs E. Constantopoulos and Son,
44 Panepistimiou Street, Athens.
Tel.: 631767.

Messrs Delta Marine Co. Ltd,
10 Venizelou Street, Athens.
Tel.: 621204.

Messrs Delmouzos and Louys,
4, Valaoritou Street, Athens.
Tel.: 631358.

John Kastrinakis,
Messrs Marine Corner,
Tourkolimanou, Piraeus.
Tel.: 473796.

Messrs Hellenic Marine Consultants Ltd,
16 Academis Street, Athens.
Tel.: 629109.

Messrs Hermès en Gréce,
4 Stadium Street, Athens.
Tel.: 237431.

Messrs Hellenic Tours S/A,
2 Stadium Street, Athens.
Tel.: 226362.

Nicos Tsouchlos,
Messrs Yachting Cruises Co.,
18 Voulis Street, Athens.
Tel.: 226840.

British Vice-Consulate:
Akti Poseidonos, Piraeus.
Tel.: 411345.

Royal Yacht Club of Greece:
Piraeus H.Q., Mounichia, Tourkolimanou, Piraeus.
Tel.: 412730.

Vouliagmeni H.Q. Marina Vouliagmeni, Vouliagmeni, Attika, Greece.
Director: Mr A. Michalidis.
Tel.: 048431.

National Tourist Organization of Greece:
Head of Yachting Section: Commander Andreas Londos, D.S.O., R.H.N. (Rtd), 4 Stadium Street, Athens.
Tel.: 220445.

British Ministry of Defence Chart Agent:
John S. Lazopoulos and Co.,
7 Astingos Street, Piraeus.
Tel.: 410625.

Engineers, Ship Repairs and Gardionage:
Messrs A. Leonidhopoulos and Company, 12k Mavromichali Street, Piraeus.
Tel.: 410264.

Ship Chandlers (who also act as agents to owners):
Messrs Speedoo Marine Ltd,
78 Akti Moutsopoulou, Zea Marina, Piraeus.
Tel.: 452557.

Electronic Equipment:
Messrs Compagnie Héllénique Radio Maritime,
26 Bouboulinas Street, Piraeus.
Tel.: 423471.

Lloyd's Agent:
Mr A. Saunders,
Navarino, 23,
Megaron Laikis, Piraeus.
Tel.: 411263.

Sailmakers and Upholsterers:
Messrs Adelphoi Trimeritis and Co.,
Tompasi Ar. 21, Piraeus.
Tel.: 483767 and 454030.

Athens Radio Maritime Station.
Tel.: 055–349.

Athens Meteorological Service.
Tel.: 980137 or 981561.

There are also agencies for the leading British yacht products, such as International Paints, Gardner and other diesel motors, Seagull outboards, etc., as well as for the various bottled gases, refrigerator and dynamo services.

CORFU

Sotiris Kaskatis, the authorized boatman, will see to most of your needs for a small unofficial gratuity. His wife will do your laundry. The engineers, led by a character called Vassili, are not all that reliable, but very enthusiastic. The slipping facilities are moderate: the shipwrights are not used to yacht work. There is an excellent electrician called Stephanos Agious (Tel.: 496). For duty-free fuel at the Yacht Station, telephone Mr Padova, the Mobil-oil agent. The taxi-drivers are mostly robbers. If I were using an agent other than Sotiris, I would favour Michael Haliokopoulos, 5 Arseniou Street, Corfu (Tel.: 8626). There is a British Vice-Consulate. The Royal Greek Navy have an information office for things like met. forecasts (Tel.: 544 or 409).

RHODES

There is an efficient Yacht Station with the usual duty-free fuel and fresh water. The harbour master's office is among the most effective in Greece. The Post Office is among the least reliable. I can recommend Messrs Frarakis and Giorgiades, N. Plastira Street, No. 18 (Tel.: 500 and 493), if an agent is required. Mr Theo Leondarakis of the Rhodes Municipal Technical School is a first-class engineer and speaks English. His telephone is Rhodes 8129. The shopping facilities are very good, with prices for luxuries lower than elsewhere in Greece, due to the special Dodecanese tariff arrangement. It is the only place in Greece I have seen English tonic water on sale. If in need of a met. forecast, Rhodes Radio Station (Tel.: 499) can probably supply one.

CRETE

Dimensions:

About 150 miles long. Maximum breadth about 40 miles. High mountains run down its middle, Mt Ida, the highest, is about 8,000 ft high. Generally very rugged. Population about 100,000.

Main Harbours:

Khania (or Canea) in the west has the island's best anchorage (also a naval base) in adjacent Suda Bay. But biggest centre is Iraklion (also called Heraklion or Candia—all very puzzling) though harbour is not so hot. The only other practical harbours—all on the north coast—are Rethimnon (don't recommend), Agios Nikolaios (pretty and well-sheltered) and Sitia, only useful as a point of departure or arrival from or to the east. All are classified as Yacht Stations of a kind.

Fuel:

Fuel easily available duty-free at Khania, Iraklion and Agios Nikolaios, also water. Water only at the other two places. Other provisions about the same everywhere.

R/T Stations:

Radio Iraklion keeps continuous watch on 2,182 kcs. Its working frequency is 2,799 kcs. Speaks goodish English and French.

Meteorological Service:

You can telephone Iraklion Met. Service on telephone number Iraklion 9499.

Make sure they give you a forecast if you want one and not just 'present weather', which is a Mediterranean habit.

Fuel and Water Prices:

The Yacht Stations will see that fuel is delivered at about 1s. 9d. a gallon and water is officially sold at 5s. a ton. Restis, the Greek petrol company, is the accredited purveyor at Iraklion and Purfina at Khania.

Iraklion Mechanics (personally recommended):

Marinakis Brothers, Iraklion (Tel.: 302).

Main Sites You Must See:

Palace of Knossos and its museum. Agia Triada Villa. Palace of Phaestos. Tables of the Law at Gortyna. Plain of Mallia.

Main Thing to Remember (even if you are unintelligent):

You are standing on the island where Europe's civilization, brought over from Egypt, first started 5,000 years ago. Experts show that it was at least as luxurious as you would have approved of. So there is no place quite like it in the world.

Turkey

Ports of Entry:

It is better to choose one of the main ports when first arriving in Turkey from abroad, although some of the lesser places will also do their best to produce the right documents. Principal ports which suggest themselves are Çanakkale (in the Dardanelles), Ayvalik (opposite Mitylene), Izmir, Kuş Adasi (near Ephesus), Bodrum (opposite Kos), Marmarice (opposite Rhodes), Fethiye, Kaş, Finike, Antalya, Alanya, Mersin, and Iskenderun (formerly Alexandretta).

Documents:

There is no document at present issued which takes the place of the 'transit log' available in other countries, so that clearance is, in fact, necessary in each port, inwards and outwards. There are prospects that this may be changed soon. In practice, regulations seem to vary greatly from port to port, but, generally speaking, clearances both inward and outward by the Health, Police and Customs are necessary everywhere.

Dues:

Again, the collection of dues varies greatly. In some ports nothing is charged, while in others not only health and port dues are levied but also light dues and extra payments for Customs overtime and Sunday movement.

Money:

The import of up to £T200 per person per visit is allowed, with the same export permitted. The official rate of exchange is about £T26 to the £, but you can get up to 50 per cent discount on this if you are lucky enough to find a bank or other place abroad which has Turkish notes to sell. Officially, one is supposed to make declarations of foreign exchange wherever one goes, but this has never, in my experience, been implemented. All the same, I always take the precaution of getting a bank certificate whenever I change foreign currency for Turkish. The best medium of exchange is the U.S. dollar note.

Passports:

No visas are necessary for British or U.S. travellers.

Health:

Technically, you are liable to be asked for certificates of vaccination/inoculation if you are thought to have come from an infected area. Practically, I have never known these be required.

Prices:

On the whole, very reasonable for all the sort of things one has to buy for one's daily requirements. Some of the more tourist-conscious restaurants are apt to ask a high price if they think you can afford it. Taxis charge normal rates, but it is essential to fix a fee first.

Repairs and Maintenance:

The Turk is a natural woodworker and charges very reasonable rates. He is not so good with metal, except for small jobs. I cannot speak with much authority about machinery, but I imagine he would be on a par with the Greek in smaller places.

Prohibited Areas:

Almost the only ones left are those in the Bosphorus approaches and those near the Dardanelles. The latter are fairly extensive and stretch from the Greek frontier to a point in the Hadramite Gulf north of Mitylene.

Charts:

The only place I know that sells British charts is at Istanbul, though it would not be surprising if there were also a chance at Izmir—but certainly nowhere else.

British Consulates:

Are established at Istanbul, Izmir and Iskenderun and are always of very great service.

Fuel:

It is impossible to get duty-free fuel anywhere. That supplied is not all that expensive and the very slightly greater sulphur content of the diesel fuel can be practically ignored.

Fresh Water:
It is getting increasingly easier to obtain, although the quality is sometimes in doubt. Charges are generally reasonable, except when it has to be brought in containers specially.

Duty-free Stores:
No facilities exist for yachts.

Ice:
Can be obtained at all the larger places, sometimes rather expensively.

Food:
Varies from very good in some of the bigger places to quite awful in the little ones. As far as shopping is concerned, the bread, eggs, meat, fruit and vegetables are invariably excellent. Wines patchy. Tinned goods very bad, so it is best to stock up heavily before leaving Greece.

Agencies:
A good agent can make a big difference to the speed of coping with the formalities and thus to the pleasure of your stay. Do not therefore avoid them altogether, but try to ensure in advance what the agency fee is to be, as sometimes this is apt to be too high. It can almost always be reduced to payable proportions.

ISTANBUL
The British Consulate-General, at least up to recently, maintained a Naval Office which we found very useful in giving good advice and by-passing red-tape.

Chart Agency:
The Sea Ship Supply Co. Ltd (Deniz Malzeme Limited Sirketti), Tophane Iskelesi Cad., No. 117, are the official British chart agents (Tel.: 495729 or 552751).

Ship Chandler:
Messrs D. F. Kounadis,
Hoca Tahsin Sok No. 17.
Tel.: 447909.

Agents:
Messrs W. F. Henry van der Zee and Co. N/V.,
P.O. Box 281, Galata, Istanbul.
Tel.: 444214 or 443904.
Mr S. Voynas is manager.

ÇANAKKALE
Messrs A. Xanthopoulos and A. Anafarta are excellent agents (Tel.: 32 and 8). I recommend leaving all clearing arrangements to them. They can also fix a taxi and military permit to visit Troy.

IZMIR
Agents:
Messrs W. F. Henry van der Zee and Co. N/V.,
Atatuerk Caddesi, 134.
Tel.: 32067 and 32068.
There is also a helpful Shell office for getting fuel. Fresh water is laid on to the quay (rather primitively).

KUŞ ADASI
Agency:
The Akdeniz Travel Agency, Banka Sokak, No. 1e, Kuş Adasi, are reliable and arrange the formalities quickly. (Tel.: 99. Cables: Akdeniz Kuşadasi). I usually pay about £2 in handling charges to the agency and port dues amount to about 10s. There is an ice factory on the quay. I usually water from the adjacent restaurant (tip). They also arrange taxis for Ephesus, etc.

BODRUM

Mr Turgut Nalbantoglu has been recently appointed Chef du Bureau de Tourisme et de l'Information. Home telephone number is 73. I suggest he should be contacted at his quayside office before committing oneself in any way. The Plaj Motel Lokanta is an excellent place for a meal and for spending a night ashore in quiet and civilized surroundings (Tel.: 83). They will send a boat for you to the quay to fetch you. Ice and fresh water available.

MARMARICE
Agency:
The Karia Travel Agency, Kordon Boyu, 43 (Tel.: Marmarice 44), is to be recommended. The manager is Mr Mustafa Girgin. Fresh water laid on to the quay. Ice available.

FETHIYE
Agent:
Mr Erol Berk (Tel.: Fethiye 32) is not an agent by profession, but is extremely helpful to yachts. He speaks English and French. Ice available. Fresh water laid on to quay. One can fuel here and the officials are unusually helpful.
Mr Ihsan Akgun, of the Government Tourist Office (Tel.: 44), can be of use.

ANTALYA
Agency:
Messrs Express Vapur Agentalyi.
Tel.: 1069 and 1698.
Mr Kayhan Ondemir.
Also Messrs Ibrahim Naccache and Co., Iskeli, 61.
Tourist Information and General Adviser:
Madame Ermin Nerkan,
Cumhuriyet Oteli, Antalya.
Tel.: 2071.

There is also a branch of the Turkish Government Tourist Agency here.
Ice and fresh water are available.

SIDE
Mr Çem Sakir Kabaagac, Manavgat/Side, Province of Antalya, resides here at the Hotel Side, which he owns with his father. He is intelligent, educated and speaks English and French fluently. He may be engaged as a guide-interpreter for local excursions and can, if required, join a yacht in this capacity.

MERSIN
Agents:
Messrs Ibrahim Naccache and Co.
Tel.: 1491.
The Turkish Government Tourist Agency maintain a branch in the town. Ice, fresh water and fuel are obtainable.

ISKENDERUN
Agents:
Messrs Ibrahim Naccache and Co. Ltd (Mr Michel Naccache).
Tel.: 1086 and 1061.
Messrs W. F. Henry van der Zee and Co. M/V. (Mr John Barbour).
Tel.: 36.
There is a British Vice-Consul. Ice is obtainable. Not a good place for fuel and water, as one has to lie at anchor.

Cyprus
NICOSIA
British High Commission. Tel.: Nicosia 73131.
The staff are most helpful to visitors, even to the extent of helping with crew, as well as shopping advice, transport, passport and visa problems, etc. It is polite to sign the High Commissioner's Visitors' Book on arrival.

FAMAGUSTA

British Compound (in the Commercial Port). Tel.: 3155.

Sea Transport Officer: Captain J. H. Davis, O.B.E.

Officer in Charge of Yachting Unit: Major Leslie Coney, R.C.T., 59 Squadron, Royal Corps of Transport.

Port Superintendent's Office. Tel.: 2748. For clearance, etc.

Transport, travel and General Agency:
Messrs Hull, Blythe and Araouzos, Ltd. Tel.: 2166.
Ask for Mr Stavros Pavlides.

Slipway:
Messrs Chrysostomos Antoniou, No. 2, 28th October Street.
Tel.: 2763 (office); 3561 (home).
Manager: Mr Andreas Tzortzios.
This firm are general contractors, also to the local British Army unit, and in addition to providing slipping facilities, will undertake all normal shipyard jobs. Slipping charges vary, but I was informed that for a boat 54 ft long, such as mine, the charge would be £70, to include one month on the ways.

Ship Chandler (paints, varnishes, etc.):
Messrs Lordos and Panayotis, Ltd, 24 Aeschylus Street.
Tel.: 3709.

Laundry:
Messrs Fotini, Kalli and Son.
Tel.: 3724.

Fuel:
Messrs L. Christofides and Co. Ltd (Shell agents).
Tel.: 2245.

Ship Chandler (stores of all kinds, incl. duty-free):
Nicos Kokkinos,

Socrates Street, 9.
No telephone.

KYRENIA

Groceries, etc.:
Messrs Neocles Loizou.
Tel.: 223.

Restaurants:
The Harbour Club (Judy and Roy Findlay).
Stan's Hide-Away.
Theo's.

Electrician:
Aggele Loizos,
Arodaphnouzas Street, 1/3.

Good Advice:
Andreas Kariolou,
Hesperides Hotel (also for eating).
Tel.: Office 389; Home 424.
Cannot do better than what he suggests.

Radio Telephone:
Cyprus Radio (stationed at Limassol) keeps continuous watch. After preliminary calls on 2,182 kcs, its working frequencies are 2,670 kcs and 3,690 kcs, preferably the former. Its strength is 0.5 kW.

Met. Forecasts:
Dhekelia radio station broadcasts weather forecasts at 0600 and at 0755 on 1,439 kcs and 1,421 kcs.

Money:
Cyprus being in the sterling area, there is no difficulty in obtaining facilities for transfers of money from England to local banks. Almost all shops will accept cheques on U.K. banks in payment.

Temperatures:
Daytime temperatures in Kyrenia, where there was also considerable humidity, usually reached 95 degrees Fahrenheit

and more in September. In Famagusta they were slightly lower and it seemed less humid, perhaps due to the afternoon sea breezes.

Ports Generally:
As far as we could gather, Kyrenia and Famagusta were the only ports offering absolutely secure harbour to a yacht, though Paphos in the south-west was mentioned as being fair. Larnaca and Limassol both appeared to offer only anchorages. There are, however, a number of smaller anchorages around the island where a yacht can lie safely in certain winds.

Gas:
Although I did not actually fill my gas cylinders in Cyprus, I was told that this would have been easy to have arranged at reasonable prices.

Lebanon
BEIRUT
Beirut Yacht Club. Tel.: 242996.
Secretary and Manager: M. Jean-Pierre Selwan.
Commodore: Dr Fred Zebouni.
Vice-Commodore: M. Henri Nakash.
Boatmen: Dimitri, Wehbe and Ibrahim —all helpful, Dimitri speaks a little Greek.

Port Captain:
Josef Badoura.

Sanitary Officer:
Dr S. Yanacopoulos.

Stores:
Messrs Smith's Supply and Trading Co., Rue Sadat, Ras Beirut.
Tel.: 223171; 248177.

Reliable English-speaking taxi-driver:
Ask for Alberto at the Phoenicia Hotel (Tel.: 252900).
An ex-seaman with good local knowledge.

TRIPOLI
Ship Chandlers:
Ibrahim Rashidi and Sons.
Tel.: 26192 and 26177.

Currency:
The rate is 8.60 Lebanese pounds to the pound sterling. There seem to be no exchange restrictions, even Turkish notes being freely bought and sold.
Prices for everything are very high.
Be careful when taking a taxi to inquire the price in advance.

Visas:
Visas are technically necessary for a British subject entering the Lebanon, even by yacht. But if he is to live aboard or at least not leave the 'precincts' of the port, he is issued with a temporary permit to visit the city where the yacht is lying. In practice this is extended to the area surrounding it.

Fresh Water and Ice:
Fresh water is of good quality and is about the only cheap thing we found in Lebanon. Ice is obtainable at somewhat inflated rates, at all ports.

Gas:
Gas bottles can be easily filled, preferably at the local French-operated Butagaz station. Prices of gas are reasonable, but beware the transport costs.

Climate:
In September 1965 the sun shone every day, but the humidity enveloped us like a great wet blanket: I am told this is normal all the summer months.

Syria

Ports of Entry:
Lattakia and Tartous (expected to open 1966).

Fuel:
There does not appear to be duty-free fuel. In Banyas I paid about 3s. a gallon for it.

Fresh Water:
Difficult to lay on and alleged to be of dubious quality.

Provisions:
We were surprised how mediocre they were.

Visas:
As in Lebanon, visas are not really required by yachtsmen living aboard.

The authorities are quite willing to issue landing permits valid for the day.

Ports:
In addition to Lattakia, ports available are Rouad Island, Tartous, Banyas (only an anchorage) and the small harbour of Jeble.

Laundry:
Good but expensive facilities in Lattakia.

Watchmen:
If the boat is empty, I recommend engaging a watchman. Fee about 30s. a day.

Currency:
The official rate of about 11 Syrian pounds to the pound sterling seems fair enough.

Index